A Manual
of the Orthodox Church's
Divine Services

Translated from the Russian
by Archpriest Dmitry Sokolof

HOLY TRINITY PUBLICATIONS
Holy Trinity Seminary Press
Holy Trinity Monastery
Jordanville, New York
2023

Printed with the blessing of His Grace,
Bishop Luke of Syracuse
and Abbot of Holy Trinity Monastery

A Manual of the Orthodox Church's Divine Services:
text ©1962 Holy Trinity Monastery

Second Printing: 1975
Third Printing: 2001

A Manual of the Orthodox Church's Divine Services:
format and revised text © 2023 Holy Trinity Monastery

PRINTSHOP OF
SAINT JOB OF POCHAEV

An imprint of

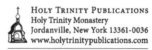

HOLY TRINITY PUBLICATIONS
Holy Trinity Monastery
Jordanville, New York 13361-0036
www.holytrinitypublications.com

ISBN: 978-0-88465-492-6 (paperback)
ISBN: 978-0-88465-497-1 (ePub)

Library of Congress Control Number: 2022950817

Cover Photo: "Censer in Church, Insense and Smoke"
Source: Dreamstime.com / ID: 213386672 / © Ivan Derkach

Contents

Preliminary Ideas

The Nature of Divine Service

By *Divine Service* the Orthodox Christian Church means a series of prayers, recited or sung in a given order, with certain ceremonies, by means of which prayers, Orthodox Christians glorify God and His Saints, express their thanks and offer their petitions, and through the performance of which they receive from God mercies and the grace of the Holy Spirit.

Divine service is *private* or *domestic* when it is performed in private by one or several persons; it is *public* when it is performed in the name of the whole Church, or of a community of Christians, by persons authorized to do so. The prayers used in public worship are divided into two categories: those for *permanent* services, i.e., services performed daily for the benefit of all Christians, and those for *occasional* services, i.e., services which are performed only on certain occasions, according to the special needs of the faithful, and therefore are called *tréba*, a word which, translated, means "need."

The Origin of Divine Service

Divine service made its appearance on earth simultaneously with man. The goodness and almightiness of the Lord impel men to glorify and thank Him; the consciousness of their wants prompts them to address their petitions to Him. And as man consists of both body and soul most closely united, therefore prayer is expressed in words and accompanied by certain motions of the body, and, vice-versa, external objects arouse a prayerful inclination in man. In this way, private worship originated and developed, varying as to prayers and rites.

But men came together and formed communities, and this gave rise to uniform prayers for all the members of one community, and for these common prayers, there were gradually appointed: place, time, order of services and persons to perform them. In this way, as human society became organized, public worship also developed.

In Old Testament times, previous to Moses, divine service was of the private, domestic type. The paterfamilias — the patriarch — on behalf of his entire family or kin (tribe), selected the place, appointed the time and laid down the order of prayer. Even then, certain customs already began to harden into rules which the patriarchs themselves observed, following their fathers' example. But since Moses' time, the Israelites had a public worship, instituted by God Himself, with temple, priests and rites. Jesus Christ, the founder and the Head of the Christian Church, while Himself complying with all the regulations of Jewish worship, did not give to His disciples any definite ritual. But He instituted the Sacraments, commanded His disciples to preach the Gospel, taught them how to pray, promised to be present in the gatherings of Christians assembled in His name, and thereby laid the foundation of His Church's public worship. Thus it was that, immediately after Christ's ascension to Heaven, a certain order of public worship gradually began to develop in the Christian community. In the Apostles' lifetime already, certain holy persons were consecrated, certain places were appointed for divine service, and a ritual was instituted for those offices during which the Sacraments of Baptism and the Eucharist are administered. Furthermore, the principal rites were devised to accompany the celebration of the other Sacraments, even to the appointing of the times for common prayer, certain feast-days and fasts. The persecutions which the Christians suffered during the first three centuries hindered them from composing an entire ritual for public worship and making it uniform for all Christians; such a ritual was fully developed and finally established only when Christianity was proclaimed the ruling religion of the Roman Empire.

External Signs Used In Divine Service

Several of the external signs of prayer are common to all men; such are: inclinations of the body, as low as the waist or all the way to the ground, kneeling, bowing of the head, lifting up of the hands. All these gestures express devotion to God, humility, repentance, supplication for mercy, gratitude, and reverence.

But apart from these universal expressions of prayerful feeling, Orthodox Christians, when praying, use a sign which belongs exclusively to them: the sign of the Cross. This sign, according to oldest custom, we make in the following manner: the thumb, the index and the middle finger of the right hand we join together, while we bend down the third and little fingers till they touch the palm of the hand. Having arranged the fingers in this manner, we touch with them first the brow, then the breast, and after that, first the right shoulder and then the left, thus making on our persons the sign of the Cross. By this sign we express our faith in the things which Christ the Saviour taught us and did for us. By joining the three fingers, we express our faith in the Most Holy Trinity, consubstantial and indivisible; by the two fingers bent to the palm of the hand we express our belief in the descent to earth of the Son of God, and in His having assumed humanity without divesting Himself of His divinity, thus uniting both natures in Himself, the divine and the human. By touching our brow, breast and shoulders, we express our belief that the Triune God hath sanctified our thoughts, feelings, desires and acts. Lastly, by making on our persons the sign of the Cross, we express our belief that Christ hath sanctified our soul and saved us by His sufferings on the Cross.

Plan of a Russian Orthodox Church of the most usual type.

A. The Sanctuary.	7. The North Door.
0. The Ikonostas (Screen).	8. The Ambo.
1. The Altar Table.	9. The Cleros (Choirs).
2. The Table of Oblations.	10. The Soleas.
3. The Bema (High Place).	11. The Nave, or Body of the church.
4. The Vestry.	12. The Vestibule.
5. The Royal Gates.	13. The Bell-tower.
6. The South Door.	14. The Porches.

The Christian Church Building

Names of the Various Church Buildings and Their Origin

We give the name of *Temple* or *House of God* to a building specially consecrated to God, or to a separate part of a building so consecrated, where Christians assemble to offer up to God their common prayers, and to receive from Him His grace through the Holy Sacraments. Because the totality of Christians taken together forms the Church, therefore the buildings in which they assemble for common prayer are likewise called *churches*.

Every church is consecrated to God and sanctified in the name of the Most Holy Trinity, and is therefore entitled "a temple or church of God." But apart from this general designation, each church has its own particular appellation, such as: "Church of the Holy Trinity," "of the Resurrection of Christ," "of the Holy Apostles, Peter and Paul," "of the Dormition of the Most Holy Mother of God," "of St. Andrew the First-called," "of St. Nicholas the Wonderworker." Special names are given to churches erected on some particularly memorable occasion, because churches are frequently dedicated to the memory of some event or other out of the life of the Saviour or of His Mother, or else of some Saint who is especially honored in some given locality, or whose name was borne by the chief founder of the church.[1]

When one town or city holds several churches, one of them receives the title of "general" or "universal" *(sobór)* because, on solemn feast days, not only the church's own parishioners, but people from all parishes assemble there for divine service also. In large cities there frequently are several general churches. That in which is situated the episcopal *cathedra* or *throne* is called *Cathedral.*

Together with the organization on earth of the community of believers in Christ, Christian churches made their appearance as gathering places for these believers. The Apostles and the early Christians endured persecution for their faith from the heathen, and for that reason used to assemble for prayer in private houses; but even in such houses they used to set apart for worship one room on which they looked with reverence, as on a place where the Lord was present by His grace. When the Christians increased in numbers and room was lacking in private houses for their gatherings, while they were not permitted to build special temples for their own worship, they began to meet together to offer their prayers to God in woods, in mountain gorges and in caves, or, if they lived in cities or in the neighborhood of cities, they assembled in the underground cemeteries known by the name of *catacombs.* So long as they were persecuted for their faith they could not decorate the places where they assembled, even though they wished to do so. Still, impelled by their pious feelings, they used, in the place of decorations, certain allegorical signs or *symbols,* intelligible to them alone. Thus, on the walls of the catacombs, they represented the Cross of Christ by the sign *T;* sometimes they drew a square block of stone and on that, a door, seeing in this a semblance of Christ, Who is the rock of salvation and the door through which whosoever passeth shall be saved. Frequently again, Christ was represented in the shape of a fish, because the Greek word for "fish," *ichthys,* is composed of the initials of the words: *Iesous Kristos Theou Huios Soter,* which means "Jesus Christ, Son of God, Saviour." Still more frequently, He is represented as a Lamb, or as a Shepherd carrying a sheep upon His shoulders. The Resurrection was depicted as the whale ejecting a man (the Prophet Jonah) out of its maw. At a later time they began to draw the portraits of martyrs somewhere about their tombs in the Catacombs. At that time, they performed divine service in garments of the ordinary cut, only they wore their best and most ornamented clothes, preferably white ones. When Christians were allowed to publicly profess their faith, they began to build temples, or churches. Sometimes they transformed existing buildings into churches, adapting them to their requirements. But they mostly erected special buildings, which differed from others both in external appearance and internal arrangement. The first churches built by Christians differed from our modern churches in that they had no screen *(iconostás)*, but the sanctuary was separated from the body of the church only by a curtain, or even merely a railing. Besides which, large extensions were added to the ancient churches for the use of *catechumens,* i.e., persons who had not yet received Holy Baptism, but were preparing to receive it and were undergoing elementary instruction in the Christian faith.

External Appearance of Churches

The most generally accepted shape for Christian churches is the *oblong,* in imitation of a ship. By giving their churches such a shape, Christians express the thought that, as a ship, under the direction of a good helmsman, carries men through stormy seas into a peaceful harbor, so the Church, governed by Christ, saves men from drowning in the deep waters of sin and brings them into the Kingdom of Heaven, "where there is neither sorrow nor sighing." Churches are frequently built in the shape of a *cross,* to show that Christians obtain salvation through faith in Christ crucified, for Whose sake they themselves are ready to suffer all things. Sometimes a church is given the shape of a *circle* in token that the Church of Christ (i.e., the community of those who believe in Christ) shall exist through all eternity and. that it will for ever and ever unite the faithful with Christ, for the circle is the emblem of eternity. Sometimes, again, the shape is that of an *octagon*—the shape of a star—in token that, as a star shows a man his way on a dark night, so the Church helps him to walk along the path of righteousness amid the darkness of iniquity which encompasses him. The latter two shapes are not so often used, as they are inconvenient for the inner arrangement of the church.

The entrance into a church is almost always from the west, the church itself being turned with its main part towards the east, in token that the Christian worshippers enter from the darkness of impiety into the light of truth (the East being the symbol of light, good, truth; while the West is the symbol of darkness, evil, error). This rule is departed from only if a building formerly erected for another purpose is changed into a church, or if a church is arranged in a private house, where the entrance and the main portion are located according to convenience.

On the roof there are usually one or several *cupolas* (towers with rounded or pointed roofs), signifying that Christians should detach themselves from earthly attachments and aspire heavenward. These cupolas are sometimes called *crests* or *summits.* One crest or cupola signifies that the community of Christians has only one head—Christ; three cupolas are erected in honor of the Most-Holy Trinity; five point to Christ and the four Evangelists, who left for us descriptions of Christ's life; while seven indicate the seven sacraments (through which we receive the seven gifts of the Holy Spirit), and the seven Ecumenical Councils, by the ordinances of which Christians are guided to this day; nine crests remind us of the nine classes of angels who dwell in Heaven, whom Christians wish to join in the Kingdom of Heaven while thirteen crests signify Christ and His twelve Apostles. Every cupola, or, where there is none, the roof, is surmounted with a Cross, the instrument of our salvation.

The Internal Arrangement of Churches

The interior of a church is divided into several compartments: (1) the *Sanctuary,* where divine service is performed; (2) the *Chapel of the Prothesis,* containing the *Table of Oblations,* for the reception and preparation of the sacred Gifts; (3) the *Vestry*, for the keeping of sacred vestments; (4) the *Body of the Church*, for the worshippers; (5) the *Vestibule* and *Porch*, for the catechumens.

The Sanctuary and Its Articles

For those who perform divine service, the eastern part of the Church is set aside. It is somewhat raised above the other portion, in order that the service be heard by all present, and is called the Sanctuary. Persons not consecrated to the service of the church are not permitted to enter this part of it. The sanctuary is divided from the worshippers by a curtain, and a partition or screen. In some churches there are several sanctuaries dedicated to the memory of various events and various persons. They are called annexes or chapels.

In the middle of the sanctuary there stands a square table; it is the altar; also called *Holy Throne*, because the Lord is present on it, or *Holy Table*, because upon it Christians are offered the Sacrament of the Eucharist, with which they partake of the Body and Blood of Christ. The altar is made square in token that Christ's doctrine and sacrament are free to men of all four parts of the world.

The altar, as being the place on which rests the Glory of the Lord, is vested with two coverings; the first is of white linen; the second or outer covering is of rich brocade. Upon the altar is laid a silken or linen cloth, on which is represented the Descent from the Cross and the preparation of Christ's body for interment. This cloth is called the *Antimíns*, which means "what is instead of the altar."

The origin of the Antimins is as follows: The law demands that a Christian church shall be consecrated by a bishop; and as there was not always one on hand to do so, and, besides, as movable churches had to be organized for travelers, it became usual for bishops to consecrate only the upper boards of the altar, or even only linen or silken cloths, which, after signing them with their name, they sent to newly-built churches, or gave to people who were starting on a journey. Later on, an Antimins became a necessary feature of every altar, even in such churches as had been personally consecrated by bishops. Into every Antimins is sewed

THE ALTAR.

1. The Tabernacle or Ciborium.
2. A Seven-Branched Candelabrum.
3. The Dikirion.
4. The Trikirion.
5. and 6. The Fans.

7. The Ciborium (to take the Sacrament to the sick).
7. The Gospel.
8. The Cross.
9. The Antimins.
10. The Altar Table.
11. A Lampada (vigil lamp).

a particle of some holy relic (i.e., of the incorruptible remains of Saints' bodies), in memory of the fact that in early times Christians used to assemble for divine service on or by the tombs of martyrs, and in token that the Saints, being near to God, intercede for us with their prayers. If the church is consecrated by a bishop, the relic is placed under the center of the altar, upon a stand in a special small casket, to keep it from injury; it is wrapped in a silken cloth called *pleiton*, which means "a wrap."

Indispensable attributes of the altar are the Cross and the Gospel.[2] The Cross is laid there as a sign of Christ's victory over the devil and of our deliverance, and the Gospel, because it is the book which contains the Word of Christ, by following which we may obtain salvation. In the first ages of Christianity, before the execution of criminals by crucifixion had been abolished, Christians used Crosses adorned with ornaments, but without the representation of Christ crucified; sometimes they painted on it only a Lamb, either standing at the foot of the Cross or carrying one.

The Gospel which is kept on the altar always has a beautiful binding, in the middle of which is a representation of Christ Saviour (mostly of the Resurrection), while the corners are occupied by the four Evangelists. These are represented with their respective symbols, in other words, their characteristics, i.e., signs which allude to the contents of the books they wrote. With the Apostle Matthew we see the face of a man or an angel, in token that Matthew describes Jesus Christ principally as the Son of Man, the descendant of Abraham, as the Messiah expected by Israel, of Whom the prophets wrote. The Evangelist Mark represented Christ as the One "Sent of God," possessed of almighty power, the King of all men, whether Jews or Gentiles, and therefore his symbol is the lion, the mighty king of beasts. The Evangelist Luke, because he represented Christ as the Saviour of all mankind, Who offered Himself as a sacrifice for the sins of men, is symbolized by the bull, the animal which the Jews used to sacrifice. The Evangelist John has given us more fully than the other Apostles the lofty doctrine of Christ as the Son of God; hence, he is associated with the eagle, the bird which soars high and fixes its gaze on the Sun.

Besides the Cross and Gospel, there stands on the altar an *ark* or *tabernacle*, in which are preserved the Holy Gifts (the Body of Christ, saturated with His Blood), reserved for giving communion to the sick, and to others at times when it is not lawful to celebrate the Liturgy. These tabernacles are sometimes made in the shape of a coffin, or a sepulchral cave, in which case they are called "Graves;" at other times in the shape of a temple. A temple-shaped tabernacle, used in old times, was called "Sion" or "Jerusalem."[3] All tabernacles alike are called *cibória*. The ciborium, used to carry the Holy Gifts into a private house, in order to give communion to a sick person, is a casket with several compartments. In one is placed a very small casket containing particles of the Holy Gifts. In another there is a small chalice with a tiny spoon, and in a third, a small vessel with wine and a sponge to clean the chalice with. Such ciboria also are kept on the altar.

The space behind the altar is called *Béma* or "high place," because it is sometimes raised above the rest of the sanctuary. On this spot is placed the *Cathedra* or throne of the bishop, and on both sides of it are seats for the priests. In our day, the episcopal Cathedræ are placed only in the principal (general) churches *(sobór)*, which hence are called Cathedrals. On the eastern side of the church above the Bema, is a representation of the Saviour, and on both sides of it, are icons of Apostles, or more often, of holy bishops. The lampada before the icon of the Bema is called *High Light*. In very ancient churches where the eastern wall always had a window, the Sacrament of the Eucharist was represented on both sides of it: on one side, Christ giving to six apostles His Body in the form of bread and on the other side, Christ giving communion to the other six apostles out of the cup filled with His Blood in the form of wine.

Sometimes a canopy is erected over the altar, on four columns, and beneath it hovers a dove with outspread wings, a symbol of the Holy Spirit.

The Chapel of the Prothesis and Its Articles

On the left-hand side of the sanctuary is placed the chapel of the *Prothésis* or "offering." That is where the offerings of Christians for the divine service are received. This chapel sometimes forms a separate compartment, divided from the sanctuary by a wall with a door, or only by columns or a curtain. In most churches, however, it is connected with the sanctuary. In this space there always is a table whereon are deposited the offerings. It is called the *Table of Oblations* and is vested with rich coverings, like the altar; the wall around it is decorated with icons. On this table are also placed the sacred vessels used in the preparation of the Sacrament of the Eucharist. They are the following:

The *Paten* or *Diskos* (which means "a round dish") on which are laid the portions of bread cut out in memory of Christ, the Mother of God and the Saints; and also for the good of the living and the dead. For greater convenience, the paten is now made with a pedestal. To it belong two small dishes or plates. On one of these plates is laid the bread, out of which a portion has been taken in memory of Christ; the top of it is stamped in the middle with a Cross, while around the rim runs the inscription: "Before Thy Cross we bow down, O Master." On the other plate is laid the bread from which a portion has been taken out in honor of the Mother of God; it is stamped with an effigy of her and the inscription around the rim reads as follows: "It is truly meet to bless thee, the Theotokos."

The *Asterisk*—consisting of two arched bands, held by a screw in such a way that they may be put together or turned around into the shape of a

Cross. It is placed over the paten, to prevent the portions of bread, which are laid on it in a certain order, from getting mixed up.

The *Spear*—A spear-shaped knife, double-edged, used to take portions out of the bread.

THE TABLE OF OBLATIONS.

1. The Cross.	7. The Spoon.
2. The Chalice.	8. The Spear.
3. The Paten and Asterisk.	9. The Table.
4. The Sponge.	10. The Censer.
5. The Ewer.	11. A Candlestick with Candle.
6. The Dishes.	

The *Chalice* or *Poterion* ("a drinking cup")—into which is poured wine mixed with water during the preparation of the Sacrament. To it belongs a small dipper, in which wine and water is presented.

The *Spoon*, with which the Holy Sacrament—the Body and Blood of Christ—is administered to communicants.

The *Sponge*—which is used for cleaning the holy vessels after the Liturgy. In our church two sponges are used. With one the paten is wiped, after the portions of bread have been dropped into the chalice; this sponge is kept on the altar in the Antimins and called "Antimins sponge." The other, which is used to wipe the chalice after it has been washed, is kept on the Table of Oblations, and is called the "cleansing sponge."

The *Veils*—one of which covers the paten, another the chalice, and a third both paten and chalice together—are used to protect the Holy Gifts from dust and insects. These veils are also called *Aërs*, because they cover the holy vessels even as air covers the earth; the largest veil is especially known under this name.

The *Fans*—are used for driving insects from the Holy Gifts when the veils are removed. In ancient times they used to be made of peacocks' feathers, linen or fine leather. At the present time they are made of metal, in the form of a circle, somewhat like the glory around a saint's head, and with a long handle; in the middle of the circle a Cherub is represented. These fans are used mainly at pontifical services, and are to remind us that Cherubim worship God with us before His altar.

The Vestry and Its Articles

On the right hand of the sanctuary a space is partitioned off and called *the vestry*. Here are preserved the church vessels, the books which are used in the performance of the services, and the vestments of those who officiate in them. As all these articles are taken care of by the deacons, the vestry is also called *diakonnicon*. In ancient times all sorts of edible gifts for the clerics used to be brought there, such as boiled rice or wheat (*kutyá*), cheese, eggs, or sweet Easter cheese (*pascha*).

The Nave or Body of the Church

The Sanctuary, together with the Prothesis and vestry, are divided from the space provided for the worshippers by a grating or screen, which is called the *Ikonostás* ("image stand"), because it is decorated with icons or sacred images. The Ikonostas has three doors. The folding doors in the middle, which lead into the sanctuary to the altar, are called the Holy Gates, because the Holy Gifts of the Eucharist are brought out through them, or the Royal Gates, because the King of Glory, Jesus Christ, passes through them in the Holy Eucharist. These doors are generally in open-work and decorated with carving and icons. These latter usually represent the Annunciation and the four Evangelists, with their symbols or characteristics, to signify that on the altar is offered the sacrifice for the salvation of mankind, the first tidings of which were received by the Virgin Mary from the Archangel Gabriel, as known to us from the narratives of the four Evangelists. Just behind the royal gates a curtain is hung. During the services the royal gates are opened for the celebrants to go in and out of the sanctuary, while the curtain is drawn across or drawn away, even when the royal gates are closed, in order to emphasize certain prayers or the meaning of certain rites. Thus, during penitential services, such as Compline, the Midnight Office and the Hours, the curtain remains drawn, in token that our sins remove us far away from heaven, from God. During solemn, joyous services, assuring us that the Lord hath saved us, such as Vespers and Matins, it is drawn away. During the Liturgy, the curtain remains drawn away almost all the time. The door on the left of the royal gates leads into the Prothesis and is called the "northern door," while that on the right leads into the vestry and is called the "southern" or "deacons' door." On these two doors there are usually paintings representing either angels—the messengers of God who minister unto Him in the Kingdom of Heaven—or sainted deacons, who in their lifetime, had charge of the Prothesis and vestry.

Besides the decorations of the doors, the entire screen which separates the sanctuary from the nave is decorated with icons, in one, two, or

1. The Ikonostas.
2. The Royal Gates.
3. The Northern and Southern Doors.
4. The Soleas.

5. The Ambo.
6. The Kliros.
7. The Banners.

more tiers. Such screens, therefore, differ in appearance: they are either like an open-work grating, varying in height, or a solid wall up to the ceiling. The icons of the first tier are called "local icons." On the right of the royal gates there is always an icon of the Saviour, and next to it the "church icon," i.e., a representation of the Saint or event, in honor of whom or which the church has been named and dedicated. On the left side is an icon of the Mother of God. In the same tier, if there is room, are usually placed the icons of such Saints as are most honored in a given locality. Above the royal gates it is usual to place a painting of the Last Supper, in token that, in partaking of Christ's Holy Sacrament, men are made worthy of entering into the Kingdom of Heaven. The second tier is the place for the presentation of the different church feasts, i.e., of the principal events in the lives of our Lord and His Mother. The third tier contains the icons of the Apostles and in the middle of them, just above that of the Last Supper, is a representation of Jesus Christ—the subject of their preaching—in royal or episcopal vestments, with His Mother at His right hand and the Forerunner at His left. Such a presentation of Christ bears the special name of *Deisis*.[4] If there is a fourth tier, it is filled with the icons of Old Testament prophets and in the middle of them is the Mother of God with the Divine Infant. A fifth and sixth tier will hold icons of holy martyrs and sainted bishops. The very top of the Ikonostas is adorned with the Cross, bearing the effigy of Jesus Crucified. An Ikonostas decorated in this manner brings before us all the denizens of heaven and serves as a book, from which even those who cannot read may learn the history of Christ's church and her doctrine.

The Ikonostas does not stand on the very edge of the raised floor of the sanctuary, but so that part of this floor projects into the nave. The part of the platform in front of the screen is called the *Soléas* (which means "an elevated place"). On this elevation Christians stand to receive Holy Communion, and the celebrants come out of the sanctuary and stand there while they recite public prayers and speak instructive addresses or read portions of Scripture. On both sides are placed the readers and singers. The middle of the platform just in front of the royal gates, where Holy Communion is administered, and prayers and addresses are read, is called the *Ámbo*, which means "Ascent," and the place set apart at each end for the readers and singers is called *Klíros*. The word means "lots." These places are called thus because in early times the readers and singers were chosen by lots.

Near each kliros are kept the portable icons, i.e., those which are used for divine services outside the church. They are fastened to long handles, sometimes by loops, more frequently by cords, and have the shape of banners. Indeed they are called banners, for they represent the banners of the church, under which Christians, being the warriors of Christ's kingdom, go forth to fight the foes of truth and love.

The space in front of the soleas is reserved for the worshippers. The walls, as well as the square pillars which support the cupolas, are decorated with icons and paintings representing events from the history of Christ's church.

Over against the royal gates, on the western side of the church, is an entrance door leading into the vestibule, and called the "beautiful door," because it usually is richly decorated — also simply the "church door," because it leads into the church. In large churches there are other smaller doors in the northern and southern sides of the church; through these the worshippers can go out into the side vestibules and to the porches.

Vestibule and Porch

The vestibule is divided into two parts, the inner and the outer, the latter being called the "porch." The inner porch, used, in the early ages, to be set apart for catechumens—persons who wished to become Christians, were receiving Christian instruction and preparing for baptism— and for penitents, for Christians who, for their sins, were refused communion. In the vestibule was placed the fount for the performance of baptism. Here, also, Christians used to take their food at a common table after the end of divine service. In some monasteries the vestibule to this day serves as dining-room or refectory. It is in the vestibules that the church orders the penitential services to be performed, in order more clearly to show that men remove themselves farther away from God by their sins and become unworthy to stand with His people. In the outer vestibule or porch the "weepers" used to stand in ancient times — a class of penitents who were forbidden to enter the church, and here implored the prayers of those who went in. In the East, funeral services over the bodies of departed Christians are held on the porch.

Articles For Divine Services

Illumination: Lampadas, Candelabra and Candlesticks

In all churches, on the Altar and on the Table of Oblations, also behind the Altar and in front of the icons, lights are kept burning, not only during evening and night services, but during day services as well. They signify that the Lord gives us the light of truth, and that our souls burn with the love of God and are penetrated with feelings of joy and devotion. It is quite in accordance with this conception that the illumination of the church is increased during solemn holiday services and decreased during penitential services.

For the illumination of a church, two things are needed: oil and wax. Oil (yielded by the fruit of the olive tree), is symbolic of grace, indicating that the Lord sheds His grace on men, while men on their side are ready to offer Him in sacrifice deeds of mercy. The pure wax, made by the honeybees from fragrant flowers, is used as a token that the prayers of men offered from a pure heart are acceptable to God.

Of the candlesticks and candelabra used in the church, some are portable and some stationary, all varying in the number of candles or lamps which they bear. The candlesticks are always portable and carry one, two or three candles. One candle reminds us that there is but one God, Who is the Light Eternal; the candlestick with two candles is called *Dikírion* ("two candles"), and indicates that in Jesus Christ are united two natures—the divine and the human; that of three candles is called *Trikírion* ("three candles"), and alludes to the three Persons of the Deity. There are stationary candelabra, standing or suspended, in front of the icons, bearing both oil lamps and wax candles. These are called *candils* or *lampadas* if they carry only one *candle; polycandils* ("many lights"), if they carry seven or twelve candles (seven candles in allusion to the seven gifts of the Holy Spirit, and twelve in allusion to the Apostles); lastly, *panicandils* ("all light") are those that carry more than twelve candles. Some times, if a panicandil is made in the shape of a circle, garnished with candles, it is called *khoros*, which means "a circle," "an assembly."

INCENSE

Besides the lampadas, candlesticks and candelabra, with their burning candles and lamps, an important item of divine service is the burning and swinging of incense (a fragrant tree-gum). This swinging is performed sometimes before the altar and the icons; then it expresses the wish of the worshippers that their prayer may ascend to Heaven, as the fumes of the incense mount aloft. Sometimes the incense is swung towards the worshippers; then it expresses the wish of the celebrant that the grace of the Holy Spirit may encompass these souls of the faithful as the fragrant cloud of the incense encompasses them. The vessel which holds the incense is called a *censer;* it is a cup with a cover running on three slight chains, which all unite into one handle.

Bell Ringing

Every church has bells. They are placed either on the roof, in the turrets of the cupolas, or at the entrance above the porch, in the so-called "bell-chamber," or else next to the church in specially erected structures called "belfries." If the bell-chamber is made in the shape of a tall turret above the porch, it is also usually called a belfry.

The bells are used to call the faithful to divine service, to express the triumph of the Church, and to announce the principal acts of the service to those Christians who are not present at it, in order that they may join mentally in the common prayers of the worshippers. There are three ways of ringing the bells, according to the object for which they are rung:

1) One bell is struck several times at short intervals. This is done before the beginning of the service, to announce that it is about to begin, and is called *the toll* In the same way is announced the moment of the Liturgy when the Great Mystery is accomplished, and sometimes the reading of the Gospel in other services. Where there are many bells, different ones are used on different days, and then they have different names — such as the "feast bell," the "Sunday bell," the "weekday bell," the "small bell."

2) Several bells are struck together three different times, in a "peal" (Russian, *trezvón*).This is usually done at the beginning of solemn services (the Liturgy, Vespers and Matins), after the single-stroke toll. On high feast-days the bells are rung in this way all day.

3) Every bell is struck once in turn, and after having gone over all the bells in this way two or three times, they are struck all together. This is called a *carillon*, and is reserved for special occasions, such as the bringing out of the Cross and the Sepulcher on Holy Fridays and during processions.

The Persons Who Perform Divine Services, and Their Vestments

The Clergy

The persons who take part in the performance of divine services are divided into *celebrants* and *church servitors*. Only those persons are called celebrants who have received the grace of the Holy Spirit, through the Sacrament of Orders: they are the bishops, the priests and the deacons.

The first and highest degree of priesthood belongs to the bishop (*Epíscopos*, which means "overseer"). This name is given to the successors of the Apostles in the service and government of the Church; with regard to public divine service, bishops are the chiefs or heads of all the churches situated in their diocese. They dedicate churches, consecrate Antiminses, give authority for the performance of services in these churches, and appoint all those who hold any office in them. During services the bishops, as the highest performers of all Sacraments through which the grace of the Holy Spirit is imparted to men, bless Christians with both hands, and, in their capacity as chief teachers and enlighteners of the faithful, also bless them with lighted candles—the *Dikirion* and *Trikirion*. When giving the blessing, they compose the fingers of the right hand in such a manner as to form the name of Jesus Christ in Greek. To accomplish this, the index is stretched out straight and the middle finger slightly bent, thus representing the letters "IC"; then the annular is bent, the thumb is laid across it, and the little finger is slightly inclined, forming the letters "XC." This way of composing the fingers is called *nominal*. In his capacity of chief over the priests, otherwise called *ieréi*, a bishop also has the title of *Arch-iereus*. All bishops are equal among themselves, owing to their common grace of priesthood. But as the districts subject to their jurisdiction differ in size and importance, as regarded in earthly kingdoms and empires, there are grades in the titles of bishops: those who have charge only of small districts or cities are called simply bishops or *Archieréi*; those whose jurisdiction extends over larger cities and provinces have lately begun to assume the title of "Archbishop" (i.e., chief, first among the bishops); the bishop of a capital city, otherwise called "metropolis," is entitled "Metropolitan"; the bishops of ancient capitals of the great Roman Empire (Rome, Constantinople, Antioch) and of Jerusalem—the cities from which the Christian faith spread over the globe—have received the title of "Patriarch" (which means "chief over the fathers").

Blessing Hand

A bishop sometimes has an assistant, who is also a bishop; these subordinate bishops are called "Vicars," i.e., "lieutenants." In some countries, as for instance in our own, the churches are governed by an assembly of several bishops; such an assembly is known by the name of "Synod."

The second degree of ordained priesthood is occupied by the *ieréi* or priests, who, by the authority and blessing of their bishops, govern small Christian communities, called "parishes," and have in their charge the parish churches. They bless the beginning of every public divine service, perform all the sacraments of the church with the exception of ordination, and have under their supervision all the persons who hold any office in these churches. They also have the right to give their blessing in the name of the Lord to those inferior to them in spiritual rank, but only with one hand. All priests are equal as regards the grace of priesthood; but there are differences among them, according to the importance of the churches and parishes committed to their care. Some are called simply priests or *ierei*; others receive the title of "archpriests" or *protoieréi*, (i.e., "first" or "senior priest"). Archpriests have the precedence when they perform services together with priests of the lower rank. The priests of churches attached to imperial palaces, to a Patriarchate, and the Synod have the title of *presbyter* ("elder") and the chief priest of such a church takes that of *protopresbyter*. Priests who have taken monastic vows are called *hieromonáchi*, which means "priest-monks."

The deacon holds the third degree of priesthood. "Deacon" means "ministrant." He ministers to the bishop and to the priests in the performance of the sacraments, but may not perform them himself, and therefore has not the right to bless in the name of the Lord. At public divine service he, by the priest's blessing, recites the common prayers, reads portions from the Holy Scriptures, and sees that the worshippers comport themselves decorously. In the degree of their ordination all deacons are equal; yet there are different grades among them. The senior deacons of the principal churches are called *protodeacons* and claim precedence when they officiate with other deacons; and the chief deacon attached to the person of a bishop receives the title of *archdeacon*. If a deacon is also a monk he is called *hierodeacon*.

Church Servitors (clerics and acolytes) are persons appointed to certain services in a church used as a place of worship. The highest position among these is that of the "subdeacons" or *hypodeacons*; they assist at pontifical services and therefore are found mainly in Cathedral churches. After them come the readers and choristers, also called "clerics" and "psalm-readers," and the sacristans or doorkeepers. Part of the latter's duty is to keep the church neat and clean and to ring the bells. During service they bring out the candlesticks and the censer, and when they have done with these duties, they take part in the reading and singing. All the church servitors together make up the "church staff," because they are attached to the church. They are also called "clerics" or, collectively, the "kliros," because in ancient times they used to be appointed by lot. Sometimes the celebrants are included in the kliros, which then might better be called the "clergy," and is divided into "higher" and "lower." The higher clergy includes the celebrants—bishops, priests and deacons; the lower includes the church servitors.

The Sacred Vestments

THE ANTIQUITY OF THE VESTMENTS

In the very earliest times of Christianity, persons officiating in a church used to wear, while performing divine service, the same kind of garments as those worn by laymen. But a feeling of reverence prompted them to appear at the common worship in clean, festive garments. The favorite color for such occasions was white, in token that church service demands holiness and purity. The garments for the celebrants were provided by the community; they were kept in secret places and given out to the celebrants when they prepared for the services. Such is the origin of church vestments or holy garments. In the course of time the cut of laymen's garments changed; various peoples adopted new fashions. However, the cut of church vestments, used while officiating in divine services, remained unaltered and universally the same, in token of the unity and immutable nature of the faith and as an allusion to the qualities demanded of the ministers of the Church. All these garments were, from the earliest times, decorated with Crosses to distinguish them from ordinary garments.

THE *STICHARION* OR TUNIC

The universal garment worn by all ancient nations, men and women alike, was the *Chiton*, otherwise called *Tunic* or *Sticharion*, a long garment with sleeves, which reached to the ground. This garment remains common to all classes of ordained persons, with this small difference that the deacon's tunic has wide sleeves, while the priest's and bishop's tunics have tight-fitting ones. By its brilliant whiteness this garment reminds the celebrant that the grace of the Holy Spirit covers him as with a garment of

THE SACRED VESTMENTS.

1. The Sticharion.
2. The Orarion.
3. The Phelonion.
4. The Epitrachelion.
5. The Cuffs.
6. The Belt.

7. The Thigh-Shield.
8. The Epigonation.
9. The Scuffia.
10. The Kamilavka.
11. The Miter.
12. The Saccos and the Omophorion.

13. The Pectoral Cross.
14. The Panagia.
15. The Orlets Rug.
16. The Crosier.

salvation and joy, and invests him with beauty. In our days, the members of the lower clergy are also authorized to wear this garment.

The Orarion and the Epitrachelion

Another indispensable portion of every man's dress was the towel or scarf, which every one wore, thrown over one shoulder and sometimes both. Poor people used it to wipe their mouth and face after ablutions; while wealthy men of rank, who had slaves to carry their towel for them, used the scarf which they wore themselves as an ornament, and therefore had it made out of rich stuffs and sometimes decorated with pearls and precious stones. Such a scarf was called an *Orarion.* The Orarion—or *Stole*—remained as one of the sacred vestments, to be used by all classes of ordained persons, in token that the grace of the Holy Spirit flows down upon them abundantly. Deacons wear it on the left shoulder and only on certain occasions bind it around their bodies crosswise. The Orarion is the deacon's principal vestment, without which he cannot officiate at any service whatever. Holding one end of it with his right hand, he slightly raises it when he invites the congregation to begin prayers and to listen attentively; also when he himself recites prayers. In old times, deacons used to wipe the lips of communicants with the Orarion after they had received the Eucharist. Because deacons minister on earth around the Lord's altar as the angels surround Him in the heavens, so, in allusion thereto, the angelic hymn: "Holy, holy, holy, the Lord Sabaoth!" formerly used to be embroidered on the Orarion. Priests and bishops wear this garment on both shoulders, in such a manner that it encircles their neck and descends in such a manner that it encircles their neck and descends in front in two ends, which, for convenience sake, are either sewed or buttoned together. From this way of wearing it, the priest's Orarion or double stole has the name of *Epitrachélion,* which means "what is worn around the neck." Priests and bishops thus wear the Orarion on both shoulders in token that they have received the added grace of priesthood and have devoted themselves wholly to the Church. Of the church servitors only the sub-deacons wear the Orarion, crossed on the shoulders or tied under one shoulder.

THE MANIPLES, OR CUFFS, AND ZONE, OR BELT

To the ancient costume also belonged the Maniples—a sort of cuffs, under which men used to gather at the wrist the wide sleeves of the *chiton* or tunic—and the *Zone* or *belt*, which they girded round their waists, when they prepared for any work or went on travels. Maniples still remain an attribute of all grades of priesthood, as an indication that a minister of the Church must hope, not in his own strength, but in the help of God. The belt is worn only by priests or bishops, and serves to remind them that God strengthens them with His own strength, places them on the path of righteousness, and helps them to ascend to the height of holiness with the fleetness of the deer.

THE *PHELONION* OR COPE AND THE *SACCOS*

Over the *chiton* or tunic the ancients used to wear a garment named *Phelónion*. It was long, wide, sleeveless, enveloping the entire person, and leaving only one opening for the head. Poor people made it out of some thick, coarse stuff, and used it only in traveling, to protect them from cold and bad weather. The rich wore the same garment, made out of soft material, so that it was not only a protection in traveling, but an ornamental cloak. It was contrived so as to enable the wearer to get out and use his hands. To this effect there were studs on the shoulders, over which were looped cords which, being pulled, shirred up the skirt of the garment. When shirred up on both shoulders to leave both hands free, it presented the aspect of two bags, one of which—the larger—hung down behind, and the other—the smaller—in front. The Phelonion has been preserved as one of the priestly vestments, in token that priests are invested with truth, and hedged off by it from all the iniquities which surround them, and consequently should be ministers of the truth. In Eastern churches the Phelonion is still made after the old model, of equal length in front and behind. But in Russian churches, where this vestment is made out of the richest cloths, of gold and silver, which it would be difficult to shirr up on the shoulders, it is cut out in front, so that it is much shorter than behind. The Phelonion is usually called simply "robe" (*ríza*).

For several centuries the Phelonion was worn also by bishops. But, when the Christian faith became predominant, the Greek Emperors granted to the principal bishops—the Patriarchs—the right of wearing the *Dalmatic,* a garment like a short tunic with short sleeves, or half sleeves, worn only by themselves and the grandees of the Empire. The bishops adopted this garment, not as a worldly adornment, but as a reminder that they must rise to holiness of life, and called it *Saccos,* which means a "sackcloth garment," or "garment of humility." In the course of time it became common to all bishops, and they wear it now in the place of the Phelonion.

THE OMOPHORION

In ancient times aged men and persons in poor health used to wear on their shoulders, over the Phelonion, to keep themselves warm, a sheepskin, which was called *Omophórion,* i.e., "shoulder covering." Some bishops, especially the more aged, wore the sheepskin even during divine service, laying it aside at the most solemn moments. Soon the Omophorion was added to the church vestments, as one distinctively belonging to bishops. It was made at first out of sheepskin, afterwards out of white woolen stuff; but now it is of the same material as the rest of the vestments. It is a long broad strip, adorned with Crosses and arranged on the bishop's shoulders in such a way that one end descends in front and the other behind. This vestment reminds the bishop that he should take thought for the conversion of the erring, as a merciful shepherd, who takes the straying sheep upon his shoulders.

THE MITER, THE SKULL-CAP (*KAMILAVKA*) AND THE *SCUFFIA*

The headdress of the ancients was a long strip of linen cloth, which was wrapped around the head and called "head-band" or "fillet." According to the position and wealth of the wearer, this head-gear differed in material and shape. At first, only Patriarchs adopted it during divine service; but in the course of time, it became a part of the sacred vestments of all bishops. At the present time, archimandrites, protopresbyters, archpriests and some priests are given the right to wear a headdress during divine service. That of the bishops, archimandrites, and protopresbyters is called a *miter* (which means "headband"); the headdresses of priests consist of one kind—the skull-cap or *kamilávka*, and the other, *scuffía*. Some archpriests are also permitted to wear a miter. The word "kamilavka" means either "something made out of camel's hair," or "something that protects against heat"; while scuffia means "something resembling a cup or a skull."

THE EPIGONATION OR *PÁLITSA*,
AND THE THIGH-SHIELD (*NABÉDRENNIK*)

In ancient times persons occupying important positions in the armies and at courts wore swords of different kinds, and under them, suspended from the belt, knee-protectors, also varying in form. They were either oblong squares, tied to the belt by two cords or strings, or smaller and lozenge-shaped pieces, tied by one string. The knee-protectors of the first kind were called "thigh-shields" (in Russian *nabédrennik*); those of the second—*epigonátion* (in Russian *pálitsa*). These articles, as well as the weapons which rested on them, were signs of distinction conferred on State servants. The Greek Emperors, after they became Christians, granted to the bishops and a few priests the right of wearing them without swords; thus they were added to the church vestments as signs of distinction. Those who receive the right of wearing the thigh-shield alone, suspend it on the right side; if the epigonation is added, the latter is worn on the right side and the thigh-shield on the left. The priests and bishops to whom these signs of distinction are granted, wear them as a reminder that they have received the spiritual sword—the Word of God—with which they must smite all that is impure and vicious.

To recapitulate: The tunic or sticharion is the garment of the reader; that of the sub-deacon is the tunic with the orarion or stole, always folded round the person; deacons have the tunic, the stole and the maniples, priests—the tunic, the epitrachelion or double stole, the maniples, the belt, and the phelonion or outer robe; and some have, in addition to these, the thigh-shield, the epigonation, the kamilavka or skull-cap, and the scuffía. The vestments of a bishop are: The tunic, the epitrachelion, the belt, the maniples, the thigh-shield, the epigonation, the saccos, the omophorion and the mitre.

The Pectoral Cross, the Panagia, the Crosier and the Orlets (Eagle Rug)

These form part of the special attributions and adornments of bishops at the present day.

They wear a Cross on their breast, outside their robes, as a reminder that they should not merely carry Christ in their hearts, but also confess Him in the face of all men, i.e., that they must be preachers of the faith of Christ. Such Crosses, ornamented in various ways, are given as signs of distinction to all the archimandrites also, and to several archpriests and priests.

The Panagia which means the "All-holy," is a round or oval image of the Saviour or the Mother of God, not large, but richly decorated, which bishops wear on the breast. It is also given to some archimandrites. In old times panagias were made of a somewhat different shape—that of a folding diptych, round or square, on one side of which was the image of the Virgin Mary on the other, that of the Saviour or of the Holy Trinity. There also was a receptacle for holding particles of holy relics.

The *Crosier,* or pastoral staff, is nowadays used by all bishops in token that they are shepherds of Jesus' flock and should care for it as a father for his children. For this reason the crosier is also called *paterissa* (from the Greek word *pater,* "father"). The episcopal crosier has a double crook on top, and above that—a Cross. The crook is usually made like serpents' heads at both ends, in memory of the Saviour's words: "Be wise like unto serpents." As the serpent is renovated yearly, casting off its old slough and forcing its way through thorny plants, so the bishop, while guiding his flock, must follow himself and lead others along the path of enlightenment and renovation, in despite of sorrows and sufferings. Below the crook, a piece of some kind of handsome cloth is tied, usually silk, as an ornament, and to make it pleasanter to the hand to hold the staff.

The *Orléts* (eagle rug) is a small round or oval rug, whereon is represented an eagle with a glory around his head, flying above a city. During divine service, the bishop stands on such rugs, as a reminder that he should, by his teaching and his life, rise above his flock, and be to them the example of a soul aspiring from the things of earth to those of heaven.

Public Worship

The Daily, Weekly, and Yearly Cycles of Services

Public worship consists of various collections of prayers, or church services. All these services are adapted to the twenty four hours of the day. They express our remembrance of events which happened at certain hours, and contain petitions suited to these memories.

THE DAILY CYCLE OF SERVICES

In ancient times, days were counted from the evening. At six o'clock p.m. (as we count time), *night* began, which was divided into the following four portions or *watches* (times of changing sentries): *evening* (from 6 to 9 p.m. as we would say); *midnight* (from 9 p.m. to 12); the *cock-crow* (from 12 to 3 a.m.); and *morning* (from 3 to 6 a.m.). The day began at 6 a.m. by our reckoning, and was also divided into four watches or hours: the *first hour* (6 to 9 a.m.); the *third hour* (from 9 a.m. to 12 or noon); the *sixth hour* (from 12 to 3 p.m.); and the *ninth hour* (from 3 to 6 p. m.). Christians began each portion of the day by common prayer. This resulted in eight services: *Vespers, Compline, Midnight Office* and *Matins* for the night; the services of the First, Third, Sixth, and Ninth Hours for the day. Besides these, in fulfillment of Christ's command to break bread in memory of Him, Christians celebrate every day the Liturgy, or, if not the Liturgy, the *Typica*, otherwise called the "Pro-Liturgy Service." Thus was formed a daily cycle of nine services

THE WEEKLY CYCLE OF SERVICES

Every day of the week is consecrated to certain special memories as follows: *Sunday*, to that of Christ's rising from the dead; *Monday*, to honoring the holy Angels; *Tuesday*, to the memory of the Prophets and, among them, of the greatest among prophets, John the Forerunner; *Wednesday* is consecrated to the Cross of Christ, as being the day of

Judas' treason; *Thursday*, to the memory of the Apostles and all sainted bishops, and, in their number, of Nicholas, bishop of Myra in Lycia; *Friday*, to the Cross, as being the day of the Crucifixion; *Saturday*, to the Saints, especially to the Mother of God, and to the memory of all those who have died in the hope of resurrection and eternal life. The remembrance of these events and persons is recalled by certain prayers and hymns, different for each day of the week, which enter into the fixed daily cycle of services. Besides which, the services for Saturday and especially those for Sunday, are celebrated with greater solemnity, as being feast-day services; while the services of Wednesday and Friday are consecrated to penance, and are accompanied by severe fast all through the year, with the exception of six weeks in the year, when the fasts are suspended in honor of special memories. These weeks are called *unbroken weeks*, because they are not broken by fasts. They are the two weeks after Christmas day, the week of the Publican and the Pharisee, the week before the beginning of Lent, the Easter week and the week following the Pentecost. Such are the peculiar features of every day of the week, and thus is formed *the weekly cycle of services.*

THE YEARLY CYCLE
Every day of every month, every day of the year is consecrated to the memory of certain events or to that of different Saints. In honor of each given event or person, special hymns, prayers and rites have been established, which are added to the hymns and prayers for the day of the week, introducing more new features into the fixed routine of the daily services—features which change with every day of the year. This forms *the yearly cycle of services.*

FEASTS
In the yearly cycle, the greatest changes in the service occur on great feast-days and during the fasts. According to the subjects of the services, the feast-days are divided into *Feasts of Our Lord*, in honor of God Himself, *of the Mother of God*, and *Saints' Feasts*, in honor of the holy

angels and of holy men. According to the solemnity of the services, they are divided into *great, medium,* and *lesser;* according to the time of celebration, *into fixed,* i.e., such as return periodically on the same dates of the same month in each year; and *movable,* i.e., such as occur yearly on the same days of the week, but on different dates and even in different months, following the movements of the Paschal Feast.

The Paschal Feast (Pascha, i.e., Easter Sunday)

The Paschal Feast, being the day of the Resurrection of Our Lord, is the feast of feasts. Besides this feast there are twelve more, some fixed, some movable, which are distinguished by services of especial solemnity. They are called the *Twelve Feasts.* Of these, some are established in honor of the Lord, others of the Mother of God. The former are: *The Nativity of Christ* (Christmas), 25th of December; the *Theophany* (Epiphany), 6th of January; the *Transfiguration,* 6th of August; the *Entry Into Jerusalem,* (Palm Sunday); the Sunday before Pascha; the *Ascension,* on Thursday, the fortieth day after Pascha; *Pentecost,* in commemoration of the Descent of the Holy Spirit on the Apostles, on Sunday, the fiftieth day after Pascha; and the day of the *Exaltation of the Holy Cross,* in memory of the finding and setting up ("exalting") for public adoration of the Cross on which Christ was crucified, 14th of September. The feasts celebrated in honor of the Virgin Mary are: her *Nativity,* 8th of September; her *Entry Into the Temple,* 21st of November; the *Meeting of the Lord,* 2nd of February; the *Annunciation,* 25th of March; and the *Dormition of the Mother of God* (Assumption), 15th of August.[5] There are days preceding and following each of the twelve feasts, during which the hymns belonging to the feast are sung at all services. Over and above this, the day following many of the Twelve Feasts is consecrated to the memory of the persons who took part in the event which the feast commemorates. Thus the day after that of the Nativity of Christ is called "the Synaxis of the Virgin," i.e., the congregation meets to do honor to the Mother of God; the day after the Epiphany there is a service in honor of St. John the Baptist; the day after the Pentecost, in honor of the Holy

Spirit; the day after the Nativity of the Virgin, in honor of her parents, St. Joachim and St. Anna; the day after the Annunciation is called "the Synaxis of the Archangel Gabriel"; the day after the Presentation of the Infant Jesus, "the Synaxis of St. Symeon and Anna the Prophetess." The Church prepares for some of the feasts by fasts and special prayers for the dead.

The substance of the hymns for the various festivals is contained in the *tropario*—or verse for the day.

Troparion for the Nativity of the Virgin

Thy Nativity, O Theotokos Virgin, hath proclaimed joy to all the world; for from thee hath dawned the Sun of Righteousness, Christ our God, annulling the curse and bestowing the blessing, abolishing death and granting us life eternal.

Troparion for the Entry of the Virgin into the Temple

Today is the prelude of God's good will, and the heralding of the salvation of mankind. In the temple of God, the Virgin is presented openly, and she proclaimeth Christ unto all. To her, then, with a great voice let us cry aloud: Rejoice, O thou fulfillment of the Creator's dispensation.

Troparion for the Meeting of the Lord

Rejoice, thou who art full of grace, O Virgin Theotokos, for from thee hath risen the Sun of Righteousness, Christ our God, enlightening those in darkness. Rejoice thou, also, O righteous Elder, as thou receivest in thine arms the Redeemer of our souls, Who also granteth us the Resurrection.[6]

COMBINATIONS OF DAILY SERVICES

In ancient times, especially in monasteries, all the offices of the daily divine service were performed separately, at the hours appointed for them. At the present time they are combined so as to fit into three services: the *evening service*, consisting of the offices of Ninth Hour, Vespers, and Compline; the *morning service*, consisting of the Midnight Office, Matins and First Hour; and the *midday service*, consisting of the offices of Third and Sixth Hours, and the Liturgy (celebration of the Holy Eucharist). On days preceding Sundays or great feast-days, the evening and morning services are joined into one, which is called a *Vigil* (i.e., "keeping awake"), and consists of Vespers, Matins and First Hour. As in some monasteries this service, beginning after sunset, lasts till daybreak, and always contains the prayers for both evening and morning; it is called *All-Night Vigil*.

If a feast-day on which the Liturgy must be performed falls on one of the days in Lent on which there is normally no Liturgy, the following alteration is made in the distribution of the services: the morning service consists of the Midnight Office, Matins, and First Hour; the midday service, of Third, Sixth, and Ninth Hours, Typica, Vespers, and the Liturgy; and the evening service, of Compline.

The Daily Services

Vespers begins with the glorification of God, the Creator of the world and its Providence, and consists of the following parts: petitions setting forth our needs; the singing of psalms and hymns, expressive of regret for the lost beatitude of Paradise, and repentance of sins; prayers for salvation, and expressions of hope in the Saviour. The penitential prayers are followed by a hymn of praise in honor of Christ, Who came into the world, then by petitions that the Lord may have mercy on all Christians and grant them spiritual mercies. The service ends with the Lord's Prayer, a hymn of praise in honor of the Mother of God, and the prayer of the Blessed Symeon the God-bearer. Thus the Vespers service is replete with memories of the Creation, the Fall, the expulsion from Paradise and the profound contrition of the best men, who found their only comfort in hope in the Saviour and joyfully hailed His coming.

Compline is the service before retiring to rest. Sleep being the image of death, this service is permeated with the thought of death, not gloomy, but illumined by the remembrance that Christ, after His death, descended into Hell and brought forth from it the souls of the righteous who awaited His coming. There are the *Great Compline* and the *Small Compline*. The former consists of three parts. In the *first* we give thanks to God for the day, and express the hope that He will grant us a restful sleep during the approaching night, and rest after death with the Saints. These feelings find expression, besides all other prayers, in the verse: "God is with us. Understand, O ye nations, and submit yourselves, for God is with us." The *second* part is penitential. The substance of all the prayers is expressed in the penitential troparia[7] which are sung: "Have mercy on us, Lord, have mercy on us; for at a loss for any defense, we sinners offer to Thee, our Master, this prayer: Have mercy on us!" The *third* part of Compline consists in glorifications of the Lord and His Saints. The substance of the prayers composing it is expressed in the Psalm "Praise ye God in His Saints," with the added hymn: "O Lord of hosts, be with us, for, beside Thee, we have no other helper in adversity; O Lord of hosts, have mercy on us!"

Small Compline is an abridgment of the Great, consisting of the third part alone. Of the first, only the Creed is read, and of the second, the penitential Psalm "Have mercy on me, O God..."

The Midnight Office consists of the prayers to be recited at midnight, in memory of Jesus Christ's midnight prayer in the garden of Gethsemane, in imitation of the angels, who, night and day, glorify the Lord, and as a reminder that we should be ever ready to give answer on the Day of Judgment to Christ, who will come unexpectedly, as the bridegroom in the night. The *Daily Midnight Office* consists of two parts: the first reminds us by its prayers of the second coming of Christ and the Judgment, proclaiming that "Blessed are the blameless in the way, who walk in the law of the Lord"; while the second part contains prayers for the dead. *The Sunday Midnight Office* consists of glorifications of the Holy Trinity.

In some monasteries, the morning and evening prayers which all Christians should read before retiring and upon arising are adjoined, respectively, to the services of Compline and the Midnight Office.

On the days on which an All-Night Vigil is ordered, the Compline and Midnight Office are omitted, except during Great Lent, when the vigil consists (in general) of Great Compline, Matins, and the First Hour.

Matins begins with prayers for the Tsar, and, after these prayers, consists chiefly in praises of the Lord (Christ the Saviour), Who hath given us not day-light alone, but spiritual Light. Therefore, this entire service is filled with memories of the time when Christ appeared upon the earth, and lived here unrecognized by nearly all men. The service of Matins is divided into three parts. *The first* part consists in the singing of Psalms expressive of penitence and hope in the Redeemer, and general prayers for mercy. The psalm-singing begins with the Doxology which the angels sang on the night of the Nativity: "Glory to God in the highest, and on earth peace, good will among men"; then is interrupted by a more direct glorification of the Incarnation of Christ: "God is the Lord and hath appeared unto us: blessed is He that cometh in the name of the Lord"; and ends with the glorification of the person or event, to the memory of whom or which the day is consecrated. The *second* part is entirely consecrated to the glorification of the Saint of the day or of the event commemorated on that day. It consists of hymns from the Old Testament, which refer to the coming Saviour, and others from the New Testament, showing that the expectations of the righteous men of old have been realized. The *third* part consists of hymns of praise and prayers for the granting of spiritual gifts to Christians.

The Hours, or *Hour offices*, is the name given to brief sets of prayers recited at the Hours which begin each of the four watches of the day, and which, to Christians, are associated with special memories. All these offices are alike in their composition. Every Hour begins with an invitation to worship Christ and consists of the reading of three Psalms. Then follow: the troparion for the day, the *Theotokion* (a hymn in honor of the Mother of God), the Lord's Prayer, the *kontakion*[8] for the day, the prayer "Thou Who at all times and in every hour...," and the concluding prayers of the Hour. But with all this similarity, the office of one Hour differs from that of another in so far that each Hour has its own Psalms and concluding prayers, to conform with the events commemorated and with the feelings, thoughts, and wishes which these memories call forth in the soul of the believer. The office of the *First Hour* commemorates the bringing of Christ before Pilate; that of the *Third Hour* commemorates Pilate's judgment of Christ, the scourging and the mocking, and the Descent of the Holy Spirit upon the Apostles; the office of the *Sixth Hour* commemorates Christ's going forth to Golgotha, the Crucifixion, the insults offered to Him on the Cross, the darkness which covered the earth; while the office of the *Ninth Hour* commemorates Christ's Passion and death.

The All-Night Vigil is the name of the service composed of Vespers and Matins, which is performed with great solemnity, especially in the parts consecrated to the memories of the day.

GREAT VESPERS

THE BEGINNING OF THE SERVICE AND THE INTRODUCTORY PSALM

The service begins with the glorification of the Holy Trinity. With the royal gates open, the church being fully illumined, the priest, standing before the altar, sayeth: "Glory to the holy, consubstantial, life-giving and indivisible Trinity;" then the deacon[9] thrice invites the congregation to worship Christ, our God and King. In answer to this invitation, the faithful—or the choir in their stead—proceed to sing Psalm 103 of David, which glorifies God the Creator and His Providence: "Bless the Lord, O my soul! O Lord, my God, Thou hast been magnified exceedingly.

Confession and majesty hast Thou put on ... Wondrous are Thy works, O Lord! in wisdom hast Thou made them all ... Glory to Thee, Lord, Who hast made all things!" The Psalm is concluded with the thrice-sung "Alleluia," which means "Praise the Lord," or "May the Lord be praised!" This Psalm beginning the series of the daily services is called *Proemiac*, i.e., "prefatory or introductory." The words of it induce the worshippers into the blissful condition of the first man, when he, innocent as yet, praised his Creator together with the holy angels. The open royal gates remind us that sin did not at that time separate men from God, while the light of the lamps and candles and the fumes of the incense symbolize the Divine Light which illumined men, and the grace of the Holy Spirit which quickened them.

THE GREAT *ECTÉNIA*

After the glorification of the Creator in the words of the Introductory Psalm, short petitions for the granting of various favors are slowly recited by the deacon, and after each petition the worshippers—or the choir in their stead—sing the response, "Lord, have mercy!" The collection of these petitions is called *ectenia*, from a Greek word which means "extended, protracted." It begins with the invitation: "In peace let us pray to the Lord" (i.e., "being at Peace with all men and undistracted in spirit"), and consists of supplications "for the peace from above and the salvation of our souls" (i.e., "that the Lord may be at peace with us, forgive us our transgressions and grant through this salvation to our souls"); "for the peace of the whole world, the good estate of the holy churches of God and the union of all" (i.e., "that the Lord may grant peace to the whole world, help Christian communities to stand firm in faith and piety, cause the divisions between Christians to cease, and unite them all into one Church"); "for this holy temple (wherein the service is performed), and for them that with faith, reverence and the fear of God enter herein." Then follow supplications for various members of the Church and the State: "For the Orthodox episcopate of the Church of Russia (or another national Church under which the service is being held); for our

Lord the Very Most Reverend Metropolitan N., First Hierarch of the Russian Church Abroad; for our Lord the Most Reverend (Archbishop or Bishop N, whose diocese it is); for the venerable priesthood," (i.e., the body of bishops and presbyters or priests who govern the Church), "the diaconate in Christ," (the body of deacons), "for all the clergy" (all persons attached to the Church, including readers, choristers, sextons) "and people," (the congregation and parishioners); "for the suffering Russian Land and its Orthodox people both in the homeland and in the diaspora, and for their salvation"; "for this land, its authorities and armed forces"; "that He may deliver His people from enemies visible and invisible, and confirm in us oneness of mind, brotherly love, and piety"; "for this city" (or town or holy monastery, wherein the Church is), "for every city and country, and those that in faith dwell therein" (i.e., the Christian population).[10] After offering up petitions for the members of the Church and the State, we pray to the Lord "for seasonable weather, abundance of the fruits of the earth and peaceful times," (i.e., that the Lord may deliver us from calamitous weather, and from airborne maladies, from bad crops, and from war); "for travelers by sea, land, and air, for the sick, the suffering, the imprisoned, and for their salvation"; "that we may be delivered from all tribulation, wrath, and necessity"; that He may "help us, save us, have mercy on us, and keep us, O God, by Thy grace." The ectenia ends by our committing ourselves to the will of God: "Calling to remembrance our most holy, most pure, most blessed, glorious Lady Theotokos and Ever-Virgin Mary with all the saints, let us commit ourselves and one another and all our life unto Christ our God." In response to these words, the worshippers sing "To Thee, O Lord." Upon which, the petitions being ended, the priest calls out aloud "For to Thee is due all glory, honor, and worship, to the Father, and to the Son, and to the Holy Spirit, now and ever, and unto the ages of the ages"; (i.e., we offer our supplications unto Thee, because to Thee, the Triune God, we owe glory, honor and adoration). In response to this exclamation of the priest, the worshippers utter the word, "Amen," which means "yes, truly is this so." This ectenia is called *the Great,* because it consists of many petitions, also *the Ectenia of Peace,* because it beseeches for mercy. It is recited in front of the closed royal gates, in token that sin has removed us from God and has closed against us the doors of the Kingdom of Heaven. The closing of the royal gates soon after the Introductory Psalm is meant to signify that the bliss of our first parents in Eden was of brief duration.

THE KATHISMATA

The Great Ectenia is followed by the singing or reading of the *kathismáta* (singular, *kathísma*). This name is given to sections of the Psalter, that book of the Old Testament in which are collected the Psalms, or sacred songs of the ancient Hebrews. The entire Psalter, containing 150 Psalms, is divided into 20 kathismata which are all read in the course of the services of the week. During Lent, the entire Psalter is read through twice in the course of the week. Each kathisma is subdivided into three *stáses,* and each stasis is separated from the next by the thrice repeated singing of "Alleluia," with the addition of the words, "Glory to Thee, O God"; whence the stases are also called "Glories." In ancient times all the kathismata were sung alternately by two choirs; hence the separate parts of them have also been called *Antiphons,* i.e., hymns sung "antiphonally," in alternate, responding parts.[11] The word "kathisma" is derived from a Greek word which means "to sit." The sections of the Psalter are so called because, in ancient times, they were followed by homilies, during which the congregation was permitted to sit. At the present time, though the homilies have been suppressed, the name is preserved because it is permitted to sit during the reading of the Psalms. At Sunday and feast-day Vespers, the Antiphon of the first kathisma is sung, containing regrets over the happy estate forfeited through sin, together with hopes of salvation The verses of the Psalms are separated by the singing of "Alleluia.": "Blessed is the man that hath not walked in the counsel of the ungodly" (Alleluia!); "Serve ye the Lord with fear, and rejoice in Him with trembling." (Alleluia!); "Blessed are all that have put their trust in Him." (Alleluia!); "Arise, O Lord, save me, O my God." (Alleluia!)

"Salvation is of the Lord, and Thy blessing is upon Thy people," (Alleluia).

THE SMALL ECTENIA

After the kathisma follows the *Small Ectenia,* which is an abridgment of the *Great Ectenia.* It begins with an invitation to prayer: "Again and again in peace let us pray to the Lord." It consists of only one petition: "Help us, save us, have mercy on us, and keep us, O God, by Thy grace," and ends with the commendation to God's will and the doxology. The Small Ectenia serves to divide one portion of the service from the next.

THE VERSES OF THE PSALMS, "LORD, I HAVE CRIED," AND THEIR *STICHÉRA*

Repentance for sins committed calls forth in the human soul entreaty for mercy. Therefore, after the kathisma, selected verses from the Psalms are read ("Lord, I have cried unto Thee, hearken unto me"), in which are expressed: in the first place, supplication from the bottom of the heart, that the Lord may hearken to our unworthy prayers, help us to keep away from evil and from evil men, and receive us among his elect; in the second place, the assurance that the Lord will hear our prayer. The last verses of the Psalms, in which is expressed the hope of salvation, are sung alternately with hymns composed in honor of the person or event to whom the service is consecrated, and assure us that the Lord accepts the prayer of those who love Him. These hymns are called the *Sticherœ* (a Greek word, meaning, "verses") on "Lord, I have cried." The last of them glorifies the Mother of God and contains the dogma of the Incarnation, whence it has the name of "the Dogmatic Theotokion," or, simply, *Dogmaticon.*

> Lord, I have cried unto Thee, hearken unto me. Attend to the voice of my supplcation when I cry unto Thee. Hearken unto me, O Lord. Let my prayer be set forth, as incense before Thee; the lifting up of my hands as an evening sacrifice. Bring my soul out of prison, that I may confess Thy name. *(Here follows a stichera.)* The righteous shall wait patiently for me until Thou shalt reward me. *(Stichera).* From

the morning watch until night, from the morning watch let Israel hope in the Lord. *(Stichera)*. For with the Lord there is mercy and with Him is plenteous redemption, and He shall redeem Israel *(His chosen people)* out of all his iniquities. *(Stichera)*. O Praise the Lord all ye nations, praise Him all ye peoples *(Stichera)*. For He hath made His mercy to prevail over us, and the truth of the Lord abideth for ever. (The Dogmaticon.)[12]

VESPERS INTROIT AND DOXOLOGY

While the last stichera (the Dogmaticon) is being sung, the royal gates are opened, in token that the hopes of the faithful have not been idle and that the Incarnation of the Son of God hath opened to them the doors of the Kingdom of Heaven. At this moment, the priest comes out through the north door, preceded by the deacon with the censer and the candle bearer with the great candlestick and lighted candle, and, standing before the royal gates, gives a blessing with the sign of the Cross towards the east. The deacon exclaims aloud: "Wisdom! Aright!" The exclamation "Wisdom!" signifies that this entrance expresses the coming into the world of the Saviour, as thus: the entrance through the north door instead of the royal gates signifies that Christ came in lowliness; the lighted candle and the censer remind us that He brought us the light of truth and the grace of the Holy Spirit; the blessing by the sign of the Cross signifies that Christ hath opened to us the entrance into the Kingdom of Heaven by His passion on the Cross. By the exclamation "Aright!," the deacon invites the worshippers to stand reverently and decorously. They, having heard in the Dogmaticon the news of the Incarnation of the Son of God, and, seeing in the priest's entrance a symbol of the mercies which we have received through this Incarnation, sing a hymn of praise to Christ, as being God. While this hymn is being sung, the priest enters the sanctuary and stands behind the altar, near the bema.

O Gentle Light of the holy glory of the immortal heavenly, holy Father, O Jesus Christ: we, having come to the setting of the sun, *(i.e., having lived to see the sun set)*, having beheld the evening light, we praise the Father, the Son and the Holy Spirit:

God. Meet it is for Thee at all times to be hymned with reverent voices, O Son of God, Giver of life. Wherefore, the world doth glorify Thee.[13]

THE PROKIMENON

After the Doxology the *Prokímenon* is recited. (The word means "foremost, principal, chief"). This name is given to a short verse, generally selected from the Holy Scriptures, which embodies the meaning of the entire service and, therefore, refers to the chief contents of the prayers, hymns, and lessons from Scripture for the day.[14] From its importance, the prokimenon is emphatically singled out of the service. The deacon calls out, "Let us attend!" The priest blesses all present, saying "Peace be unto all!," to which the worshippers respond with an obeisance, "And to thy spirit," *(i.e., we wish the same to thy soul)*. The deacon once more calls out, "Let us attend! Wisdom!" *(i.e., let us be attentive, for words of wisdom will be spoken)*. The prokimenon is then sung three times. After which the royal gates are closed.

THE PAREMIA

On certain days, the prokimenon is followed by the reading of *paremía*. This word means "parable" or "allegory." In church services, the name is given to selected lessons or readings from the Scriptures, principally from the Old Testament, containing the prototype of the commemorated event or a prophecy concerning the same, or else explaining the meaning of the feast, or praising the Saint in whose honor the feast is instituted. Paremia are prescribed for all feast-days except Sundays, and for the days of Lent. They differ as to number. Usually two or three are read.[15]

THE TRIPLE ECTENIA AND THE ECTENIA OF SUPPLICATION

After glorifying Christ as God, we offer up our petitions in the words of two ecteniæ, spoken by the deacon: in the first we entreat mercy for all Christians, while in the second we specify what mercies we desire for their souls. The former is called the *Triple Ectenia* because "Lord, have mercy!" is sung thrice after each petition. The other is called the *Ectenia of Supplication,* because the response to each petition is, "Grant [this], O Lord!"

The Triple Ectenia begins with the invitation: "Let us say with our whole soul, and with our whole mind let us say," and consists of petitions for our Emperor,[16] for his prosperous rule, (the preservation of his life, his peace of mind, happiness, salvation; "that the Lord may specially aid and assist him in all things, and subdue under his feet every foe and adversary; for the reigning House; for the most Holy Synod, the local bishop, and all our brethren in Christ; for the Christian army; for the blessed and ever-remembered founders of this holy Temple *(in which the service is performed),* and of all our Christian fathers and brethren that have gone to their rest and lie here *(buried around the church)* (and in all other places); for mercy, life, peace, health, salvation, protection, forgiveness and remission of sins for the servants of God, the brethren of this holy Temple, (i.e., *the Parishioners of the church),* those that bring forth fruit *(who make donations)* and do good work (i.e., *bring gifts for the adorning of the church, or do other works for the good of the parish)* in this holy and most venerable church, that labor (for *the good of the church),* that sing, and for the people that stand here before Thee and await of Thee great and abundant mercies." The priest concludes these petitions with a Doxology, in which he explains that we hope to obtain from God what we ask, because He is "merciful and a man-loving God."

The Ectenia of Supplication begins with the invitation: "Let us complete our evening prayer unto the Lord" and consists of petitions that the Lord may grant us: "that the evening may be perfect, holy, peaceful and sinless; an Angel of peace, a faithful guide, a guardian of our souls and bodies; forgiveness and remission of our sins and transgressions; what is good and profitable for our souls, and peace for the world; that the remaining part of our life may be spent in peace and repentance; a Christian end to our life, painless, blameless, peaceful, and a good account of ourselves before the dread judgment-seat of Christ." In the concluding exclamation the priest again proclaims that we hope to obtain from God what we ask because He is "merciful and man-loving." In confirmation of this hope, the priest, after the conclusion of the ectenia, blesses the congregation, saying, "Peace to all," whereto the latter responds by the good wish, "And to thy spirit." After the ectenia, hymns are chanted in honor and memory of the person or event to which the services of the day are dedicated. These hymns are separated by verses taken from various parts of the Scriptures and are, therefore, called *Sticheræ on Verses*.

CONCLUSION OF VESPERS

Filled with hope in the Son of God, Who, having become incarnate from the Virgin Mary, gave to those that believe in Him the right to call God their Father, we can retire to rest without fear, even though this rest could pass into that of death. Therefore we conclude our evening prayers with the last prayer of the blessed Symeon, the Lord's Prayer, a hymn in praise of the Mother of God, and ask God's blessing, exclaiming: "Blessed be the name of the Lord, henceforth and forever more." In reply to this, the priest blesses the people, saying: "The blessing of the Lord be upon you, by His grace and love toward mankind, always, now, and ever, and unto the ages of ages."

St. Symeon's Prayer

Now lettest Thou Thy servant depart in peace, O Master, according to Thy word, for mine eyes have seen Thy salvation, which Thou hast prepared before the face of all peoples; a light of revelation for the Gentiles, and the glory of Thy people Israel.[17]

THE *LITIÁ* AND THE BLESSING OF THE LOAVES (*ARTOKLASIA*)

Sometimes, at an All-night Vigil, towards the end of Vespers, the officiating clergy go forth with censers and candles into the vestibule of the church, there to perform the *Litiá*. The word means "earnest supplication." In ancient times this was done in order that the catechumens and penitents who stood in the vestibule might participate in the gladness of the festival. The faithful used to come out with the clergy, to signify their humility and their brotherly love towards those who had sinned. At the present time this custom still survives and serves as a reminder to all Christians that they may have a care to the purity of their souls, which alone makes them worthy to enter into the House of God. The Litia consists chiefly of an ectenia, recited by the deacon, "for the salvation of the people; for the sovereign and his House; for the clergy; for all afflicted Christian souls *(afflicted by sorrow or sin)*, desirous of aid; for the city, the country and all Christians living therein; for the deceased fathers and brethren; for deliverance from famine, epidemics, earthquakes, flood, fire, sword, hostile invasion and civil strife." After the ectenia, all present bow their heads and the priest says a prayer in which he beseeches the Lord to "accept our prayer, to grant us the remission of our transgressions, to chase away from us every foe, to keep our life in peace, to have mercy on us and to save us." In the churches which have no vestibule, the Litia is performed inside the church, by the western entrance. In times of public calamities, the Litia is sometimes performed out of doors, on fields, public squares or city halls. For this purpose the clergy come out bearing Crosses, banners and icons, forming a procession.

After the Litia, the clergy, to the singing of verses, return from the vestibule into the church, and stand in the middle of it, before a table on which have been placed five loaves of bread and three vessels, one with wheat, one with grape wine and one with oil. After reading the concluding prayers of the Vespers office, the priest makes the sign of the Cross over the loaves and prays the Lord that He may bless them and multiply them "in the whole world, and sanctify the faithful (Christians) who partake of these gifts." The service concludes with the blessing of the congregation. In ancient times, immediately after the blessing of the loaves, a portion of the *Apostle* (that portion of the New Testament which contains the Acts of the Apostles, The Epistles, and the Book of Revelation) was read, with appropriate explanations. During this reading all sat, and the deacons distributed to each of the hearers a piece of the blessed bread and a cup of the wine, that they might sustain their strength. At the present time, the services being abridged, no food is offered between Vespers and Matins.

MATINS

THE SIX PSALMS
At an All-Night Vigil, Matins begin immediately after the blessing of the congregation by the priest. The church is dimly illumined and the royal gates are closed, while the reader utters thrice the Angelic Hymn, which was sung on the night of the Nativity before dawn: "Glory to God in the highest, and on earth peace, good will among men," then slowly reads six Psalms (3, 37, 62, 87, 102 and 142), in which are expressed alternately the sorrow of a soul repenting of its sins (37, 87 and 142), and hope in the mercy of God and salvation (3, 62 and 102). While the three last Psalms are read, the priest, standing before the royal gsates, secretly—i.e., inaudibly, to himself—recites the morning prayers, as the advocate of the people before the Lord.

THE GREAT ECTENIA, "GOD IS THE LORD" AND THE KATHISMATA
After the Six Psalms, we offer up to God our petitions for the granting of spiritual and bodily mercies in the words of the Great Ectenia, then we sing a hymn of praise to God, Who hath descended to earth for our salvation, a continuation of the Angelic Hymn: "God is the Lord and hath appeared unto us; blessed is He that cometh in the name of the Lord." To this hymn is added the troparion for the feast, as a reminder of the mercies bestowed upon us through the incarnation of the Son of God. While the hymn "God is the Lord" and the troparion are being sung, the illumination of the church is increased to signify that Christ, having come, is the Light of the world. The troparion is followed by the kathismata in their order, expressing, in the words of the Psalms, our consciousness of our unworthiness before God. In ancient times the lesson from the Apostle was expounded after the reading

of the kathismata. Now the latter are followed immediately by the Small Ectenia.

This part of the Matins office, consisting of a long continued reading of Psalms, interspersed only with brief Doxologies in honor of Christ's coming into the world, and in memory of the mercies which He brought by His coming, remind us of the time when Christ already lived on the earth, but was recognized by almost no one, while men went on waiting for His coming and prayed to God for mercy, listening in doubt and perplexity to the news that the Lord had already appeared upon the earth. Consisting, as it does, principally of penitential prayers, this part of the Matins office takes place with the royal gates closed.

THE POLYELEOS

The second part of the service, consisting of glorifications of the event or person commemorated on the day, is performed with especial solemnity on the vigils of feast-days. After the kathismata have been read, with the royal gates open, Psalms 134 and 135, which begin, "Bless ye the name of the Lord," are sung, with the response "Alleluia!" after each verse. This singing is called *Polyeleos*, i.e., "of many mercies," also "oil-abounding," because the words "His mercy endureth forever" are frequently repeated in it, and while it is being sung all the lights are lit. At the same time, in token of reverence and festivity, censing goes on in the whole church.

THE MAGNIFICATION AND THE SUNDAY TROPARIA

On great feast-days after the Polyeleos, standing before an icon laid on a lectern in the middle of the church, the clergy sing a short verse magnifying the person or event celebrated. On Sundays the troparia of the Resurrection are substituted for this verse; they speak of the Resurrection of Christ and invite the faithful to worship the Most Holy Trinity. These troparia are sung with the response, "Blessed art Thou, O Lord, teach me Thy statutes," and end with a hymn in honor of the Mother of God (Theotokion).

Sunday Troparia

The assembly of Angels was amazed, beholding Thee numbered among the dead; yet, O Saviour, destroying the stronghold of death, and with Thyself raising up Adam, and freeing all from Hades.

Why mingle ye myrrh with tears of pity, O ye women disciples? Thus the radiant Angel within the tomb addressed the myrrh-bearing women: behold the tomb and understand, for the Saviour is risen from the tomb.

Very early the myrrh-bearing women hastened unto Thy tomb lamenting, but the Angel stood before them and said: The time for lamentation is passed; weep not, but tell of the Resurrection to the Apostles.

The myrrh-bearing women, with myrrh came to Thy tomb, O Saviour, bewailing, but the Angel addressed them saying: Why number ye the living among the dead, for as God He is risen from the tomb.

Let us worship the Father, and His Son, and the Holy Spirit, the Holy Trinity, one in essence, crying with the Seraphim, Holy, holy, holy art Thou, O Lord.

In bringing forth the Giver of Life, thou hast delivered Adam from sin, O Virgin, and hast brought joy to Eve instead of sorrow; and those fallen from life hath thereunto been restored, by Him Who of Thee was incarnate, God and Man.[18]

THE ANTIPHONS AT MATINS

The Magnification or Sunday troparion and the Little Ectenia are followed by the singing of the *Antiphons* alternately by two choirs. They are different for every Sunday, eight in all, this being the number of chants or tones.

The following Antiphons are sung more frequently than any others:

From my youth, many passions war against me; but do Thou, Thyself defend and save me, O my Saviour.

Ye haters of Sion[19] shall be shamed by the Lord; for, like grass, by fire shall ye be withered.

In the Holy Spirit every soul is quickened, and through cleansing is exalted and made radiant by the Triple Unity in a hidden, sacred manner.[20]

THE GOSPEL

After the Antiphons comes the lesson or reading from the Gospels. In order to arouse the worshippers to attention and reverence, the deacon calls out, "Let us attend!" and thereupon a prokimenon is sung, which indicates the substance of the coming lesson or reading, after which the deacon invites the faithful first to praise God, in the words, "Let every breath praise the Lord," then to pray that, "the Lord may make us worthy to hear the Holy Gospel," and lastly calls out, "Wisdom! Aright!" The priest then blesses the worshippers and announces from which Evangelist the lesson will be read. In response to this the worshippers sing, "Glory to Thee, our God, glory to Thee!" Just before the reading the deacon once more invites attention by calling out, "Let us attend!" Then the priest begins the reading, on Sundays in the Sanctuary before the altar, and on feast-days in the middle of the church before the icon of the feast. The Gospel lesson is adapted to the event commemorated on each given day. On Sundays, the lessons selected for Matins are those that speak of Christ's Resurrection and His apparition after the Resurrection. After the reading of the Gospel lesson, the following hymn is sung:

> Having beheld the resurrection of Christ, let us worship the holy Lord Jesus, the only Sinless One. We worship Thy Cross, O Christ, and Thy holy resurrection we hymn and glorify for Thou art our God, and we know none other beside Thee. We call upon Thy Name. O come, all ye faithful, let us worship Christ's holy resurrection; for behold, through the Cross joy hath come to all the world. Ever blessing the Lord, we hymn His resurrection; for having endured crucifixion, He hath destroyed death by death.[21]

VENERATION OF THE GOSPEL OR THE ICON, AND ANOINTING WITH OIL

After the Gospel lesson, if the day is a feast-day, veneration is paid to the icon of the feast which is laid on a lectern in the middle of the church; if it is a Sunday, the Gospel is brought into the middle of the church. The worshippers reverently meet the sacred Book, as if it were Christ Himself, and sing a hymn in honor of Him Who was crucified and rose from the dead. During the singing, the faithful pay reverent obeisance to the sacred Book and press their lips to it, as being the living Word of Christ.

If the loaves were blessed earlier in the service, the brow of the faithful is anointed with oil, with the words: "In the name of the Father, and of the Son, and of the Holy Spirit!" in token that the mercy of God is vouchsafed to them, and as a reminder that the Lord demands from them acts of mercy.

The veneration of the Gospel or icon ends with a hymn, entreating the Lord to have mercy on us according to His great mercy (Psalm 50), and according to the prayers of the Apostles and of the Mother of God. The deacon asks for the granting of this same mercy in the prayer, "Save, O Lord, Thy people, and bless Thine inheritance."

As the Sunday troparia, the Magnifications, the Antiphons, and the Gospel lesson are closely connected with one another and with the verses of the Polyeleos Psalm, and are chanted only when that Psalm is sung, this whole portion of the service is sometimes called *Polyeleos*. Thence the expression, "a service with the Polyeleos," signifies that at the Matins in question there will be a lesson or reading from the Gospel.

THE SCRIPTURAL ODES AND THE CANON

After the Polyeleos, nine *odes* from Holy Scripture are sung, in which Old Testament saints expressed their hope in a Saviour and their readiness to receive Him. To these odes are added the nine odes of the *Canon*. The word "canon" signifies "rule," "order," and the name is given to a collection of verses (troparia) in honor of the event or person commemorated, composed after one definite rule, namely: each canon is divided into nine parts called odes, each of which consists of several short verses or troparia. The simultaneous singing of the scriptural odes and the odes of the canon proceeds after the following established order: first a verse from an Old Testament ode is chanted, then a troparion of the canon; after that, the next verse and the second troparion, and so forth to the end. As the first troparion of every canonic ode serves as a link between an Old Testament ode and a New Testament ode, its contents are always taken from the former. Either the event celebrated in the Old Testament ode is shown to be the prototype of that of the New Testament, or else single expressions are borrowed from the Old Testament. Hence the first troparion of each canonic ode is called *Eirmos* (i.e., "link"). The following verses of the canonic ode are called *troparia* (i.e., "verses that turn"), because, by their meter and tone, they *turn* towards their eirmos and conform to it. After each ode of the canon coupled with the Old Testament ode, the eirmos is chanted again by two choirs, which, for that purpose, come out into the middle of the church. From this manner of singing, this eirmos is called the *Katavásia* (i.e., "descent" from the soleas where the choirs are placed).

In order to shorten the service, it is usual to sing only the odes of the canon, omitting the Old Testament odes, except the ninth, since their contents are found in the eirmos of the canon. In these odes, refrains are introduced between the troparia of the canon—petitions or praises addressed to the person in whose honor the canon is composed.

The first Old Testament ode is the song in which Moses gave thanks after the passage of the Red Sea, and the submersion of Pharaoh's army. With this ode is coupled the eirmos of the first ode of the canon, in which this passage is presented as the prototype of our salvation from sin through the waters of baptism, and Jesus is glorified, Who led us out of death into life, saving us from the abyss of sin, from the slough of iniquity.

The *second* Old Testament ode is the song in which Moses exhorted the people before his death. It is sung only in Great Lent.

The *third* Old Testament ode is the song of Hannah (Anna), the mother of the Prophet Samuel, in which she gave thanks to God for having taken from her the disgrace of barrenness and given her a son. The eirmos of the third ode of the canon points to this event as a type of man who, having been tainted with sin, but having become Christian, was given the strength to bring forth rich fruits of good works, and glorify God in Hannah's words.

The *fourth* Old Testament ode is the song of the Prophet Habakkuk (Abbachum), who, under the gaze of the blazing sun rising from behind the forest-clad mountain, symbolizes the coming of Christ. The eirmos of this fourth ode of the canon celebrates the Incarnation of Christ from the Virgin Mary in the words of the Prophet Habakkuk.

The *fifth* Old Testament ode is that of the Prophet Isaiah which symbolizes the glorious coming of the Saviour as the all-vivifying light which raises the dead to life. The eirmos of the fifth ode of the canon celebrates Christ as the Light which delivers us from the darkness of sin.

The *sixth* Old Testament ode is the song of the Prophet Jonah, who was swallowed by the whale, expressing his hope to be saved by God. In the eirmos of the sixth ode of the canon, the Prophet Jonah is represented now as the prototype of Christ, risen from the dead on the third day, now as a symbol of the human race, swallowed by the spiritual Beast (the devil) drowning in the sea of life, in the tempest of sins, and finding in the Saviour alone a peaceful harbor, in which mankind is secure from the deep of evil.

The *seventh* and *eighth* Old Testament odes are the songs of the three youths, cast by Nebuchadnezzar into the burning fiery furnace. In these songs they first besought God to forgive their transgressions, then glorified Him for their miraculous preservation. In the eirmoi of the corresponding odes of the canon, the deliverance of the three youths is made to symbolize the miraculous incarnation of Christ, and the Saviour is glorified in their words.

The *ninth* ode is from the New Testament. It is the song of the Virgin Mary, in which she expresses her joy at her meeting with Elizabeth after the Annunciation: "My soul doth magnify the Lord, and my spirit hath rejoiced in God my Saviour." This ode is coupled with that of Zachariah on the birth of his son John the Forerunner. When this ode is sung, the verses are separated by the chant: "More honorable than the Cherubim, and beyond compare more glorious than the Seraphim, who without corruption gavest birth to God the Word, the very Theotokos, thee do we magnify." The Virgin's song is never omitted, except on the great Twelve Feast days, when various other texts are substituted for it. The eirmos of the ninth ode of the canon celebrates the Mother of God and the Incarnation of Christ.

In this manner the eirmoi of the canon celebrate the coming of Christ in the words of the Old Testament saints who awaited it, while the troparia glorify the Lord in connection with the event or the Saint in whose honor the canon is composed. The canon is sung with the royal gates closed, because New Testament events are celebrated therein under cover of the Old Testament.

The chanting of the canon is divided into three parts by reciting the Small Ectenia[22] after the third, sixth and ninth odes. With the canon ends that part of the service which is devoted to commemorating the special features of the day.

THE PSALMS OF PRAISE, AND THE STICHERA ON "THE PRAISES"
The third and last part of Matins consists of hymns of praise in honor of the Lord and petitions for the granting of spiritual mercies to all Christians. After the canon are chanted the Psalms 148, 149 and 150, which invite all God's creatures to praise the Lord, and are, therefore,

called the "Psalms of Praise:" "Let every breath praise the Lord"; "Praise the Lord from the heavens; praise Him in the highest; praise Him, all ye His angels; praise ye Him, all ye His hosts." On Sundays the deacon calls out before these Psalms are sung: "Holy is the Lord our God," as an invitation to begin the song of praise. Between the verses are sung hymns in honor of the event or person commemorated; these are called the sticheræ on "the Praises." The Psalms of Praise end with a hymn in honor of the Virgin Mary (*Theotokion*).[23]

THE GREAT DOXOLOGY

After the Psalms of Praise with their sticheræ have been chanted, the royal gates are opened, and the priest calls out, "Glory to Thee Who hast shown us the Light," thus inviting the faithful to glorify God for having given us the Light of the spirit — Christ Saviour, Who came into the world to illumine mankind, which had theretofore lived in the darkness of superstitions and iniquities. In those places where the All-night Vigil really lasts all night, and where Matins, being performed separately from Vespers, begins very early, the priest utters these words at sunrise and thereby invites the faithful to glorify God for the gift, not of the spiritual light alone, but also of the material light. In answer to the priest's invitation, the faithful sing the Doxology which begins with the Angelic Song: "Glory to God in the highest, and on earth peace, good will among men," and ends with the Trisagion: "Holy God, Holy Mighty, Holy Immortal, have mercy on us." This Doxology is called "the Great" to distinguish it from "the Lesser Doxology," which precedes the Six Psalms.

The Great Doxology

Glory to God in the highest, and on earth peace, good will among men. We praise Thee, we bless Thee, we worship Thee, we glorify Thee, we give thanks to Thee for Thy great glory. O Lord, Heavenly King, God the Father Almighty; O Lord, the Only-begotten Son, Jesus Christ; and O Holy Spirit. O Lord God, Lamb of God, Son of the Father, that takest away the sin of the world, have mercy on us; Thou that takest away the sin of the world, receive our prayer; Thou that sittest at the right hand of the Father, have mercy on us. For Thou only art holy, Thou only art the Lord, Jesus Christ, to the glory of God the Father. Amen.

Every day will I bless Thee, and I will praise Thy name for ever, yea, for ever and ever.

Vouchsafe, O Lord, to keep us this day without sin. Blessed art Thou, O Lord, the God of our fathers, and praised and glorified is Thy name unto the ages. Amen.

Let Thy mercy, O Lord, be upon us, according as we have hoped in Thee.

Blessed art Thou, O Lord, teach me Thy statutes. *(Thrice.)*

Lord, Thou hast been our refuge in generation and generation. I said, O Lord, have mercy on me, heal my soul, for I have sinned against Thee. O Lord, unto Thee have I fled for refuge, teach me to do Thy will, for Thou art my God. For in Thee is the fountain of life, in Thy light shall we see light. O continue Thy mercy unto them that know Thee.

Holy God, Holy Mighty, Holy Immortal, have mercy on us. *(Thrice.)*

Glory to the Father, and to the Son, and to the Holy Spirit, both now and ever, and unto the ages of ages. Amen.

Holy Immortal, have mercy on us.

Holy God, Holy Mighty, Holy Immortal, have mercy on us.[24]

END OF MATINS AND THE FIRST HOUR

Having celebrated the glory of God, we offer up petitions for all Christians and ask for spiritual mercies in the words of the Triple Ectenia and the Ectenia of Supplication, after which the Dismissal is made.

After the Vigil is concluded the office of the First Hour is read, which ends with a hymn in honor of the Virgin *(Theotokion):*

To thee, the Champion Leader, we thy servants dedicate a feast of victory and of thanksgiving as ones rescued out of sufferings, O Theotokos; but as thou art one with might which is invincible, from all dangers that can be do thou deliver us, that we may cry to thee: Rejoice, thou Bride Unwedded![25]

DAILY VESPERS AND MATINS

The daily services of Vespers and Matins differ from the same services when performed at an All-night Vigil. The daily Vespers service differs from that performed at a feast-vigil in the following points:

(1) The Introductory Psalm is read with the royal gates closed, not open; (2) The kathismata are read right along, without the chanted Alleluia after each verse; (3) There is no Vespers or evening entry, but the hymn "O Gentle Light" is recited or sung quickly, with the royal gates closed; (4) The paremiæ are omitted (excepting in Lent), as are the Litia and the Blessing of the Loaves. The Vespers service is followed by the Small Compline.

The daily Matins service begins with two Psalms, two troparia, a Theotokion, and an abridged Triple Ectenia. All these contain petitions that the Lord may, through the intercession of the Mother of God, save the Church authorities, and render them victorious over their enemies. In olden times, in Orthodox kingdoms, these prayers were offered for the Tsar. In the further order of the daily Matins service there are the following differences from the same service as performed at a feast-vigil:

(1) There is no Polyeleos or Gospel lesson, and immediately after the kathismata Psalm 50 is read, "Have mercy on me, O God!", which is followed by the scriptural odes and the canons; (2) The Doxology is recited, not chanted; (3) After the ectenia, Dismissal is not made, but the reading of the First Hour begins at once. When Matins is performed apart from Vespers, it is preceded by the Midnight Office.

The Liturgy

Concerning the Liturgy

In ancient times the name of "liturgy" was given to any common business conducted on a community's contributions. Christians very early came to give the name to that church service during which the Sacrament of the Eucharist is performed, and which is entirely pervaded with memories of the life of Christ Saviour, from His nativity to His ascension to Heaven, because at this service gifts are offered to God which have been contributed by the Christian community. It is also called the *Eucharist* (i.e., "Thanksgiving") because it expresses our attitude to Christ for our salvation, and again by a Russian word, *obiédnia*, from the fact that it is celebrated before the noonday meal, *obiéd*.

The Sacrament of the Eucharist was instituted by Jesus Christ Himself. At the Last Supper He gave Communion to His disciples, having them partake of His Body and Blood under the guise of bread and wine, and commanded them to do this in memory of Him. The Apostles held this commandment of their Master and Lord sacred. When they met together, they spent the time in prayer, in the singing of sacred hymns, and the breaking of bread in memory of Christ, i.e., they celebrated the Sacrament of the Eucharist. Already in the Apostles' time, the main order of the prayers and rites of the Liturgy was established among the Christians by oral tradition. In the fourth century, AD, the service of the Liturgy was written down both by St. Basil the Great, Archbishop of Cæsarea in Cappadocia, and by St. John Chrysostom ("the Golden-Mouthed"), Archbishop of Constantinople, as it was performed in their time with the addition of several prayers, composed by these prelates. Very few new hymns entered subsequently into the Liturgy. In this manner it came to pass that there are two liturgical rites: the rite of St.

John Chrysostom and that of St. Basil the Great; but they are very nearly identical.

As the Liturgy is a service connected with a Sacrament, not only is the order of it strictly prescribed, but also the choice of celebrants, and the time and place of celebration.

The Liturgy can be celebrated only by a bishop or a priest; and neither a bishop nor a priest may celebrate more than one Liturgy in one day. The celebrant must necessarily take holy communion himself, and for that act he must prepare himself.

The Liturgy can be celebrated only in a church, at an altar on which there is an Antimins consecrated by a bishop (see p. 10). Not more than one Liturgy may be celebrated at one altar, with one Antimins, in one day.

The time appointed for the celebration of the Liturgy is, by ancient custom, the ninth hour of the morning. It may sometimes begin either earlier or later, but never earlier than daybreak, nor later than noon, except on the days when the Liturgy is combined with the Vespers service.

The service of the Liturgy is divided into three parts: in the first, the elements for the Sacrament are prepared; in the second, the worshippers prepare to take part in the celebration of the Sacrament; in the third, the Sacrament itself is performed.

1. The Proskomédia

The first part of the Liturgy is named *Proskomédia*, which means "the bringing of gifts." It is so named because in ancient times, the elements of the Sacrament of the Eucharist were selected out of the voluntary offerings of the Christians, while at the present time they are purchased with money contributed by Christians. It is performed by a priest, robed in the full vestments of his dignity.

The elements of the Sacrament are bread and wine. The bread must be made of wheat flour, mixed with plain water, leavened, well baked, fresh and clean, neither musty nor stale. These loaves are called *prósphora*, i.e. "oblations." Each consists of two smaller round loaves superposed, indicating that in Jesus Christ two natures are united, the divine and the human. On the top of each loaf is stamped a Cross, with the following Greek inscription in the four corners: IC. XC. HL. KA., signifying "Jesus Christ prevails." Five loaves are used in the preparation of the Sacrament. The wine must be made of the juice of the grape, without admixture, neither sour nor sharp, neither mildewed nor yet rancid.

Taking up the first loaf, the priest makes the sign of the Cross on it with the spear, saying, "In memory of our Lord, and God, and Saviour, Jesus Christ"; then he cuts out a cube of the size of the entire stamp, uttering at the same time the words of the Prophet Isaiah, in which he speaks of the Saviour as of a Lamb Which takes on Itself the sins of the world. This portion is called the Lamb, and represents Christ, of whom the Paschal Lamb was the prototype. The priest lays the Lamb in the middle of the paten, makes an incision on it in the form of a Cross,

The Holy Bread which is the Lamb.

For the Most-Holy Theotokos.

The 9 ranks.

For the living.

For the dead.

remembering that Christ also, like unto a lamb, offered Himself as a sacrifice for the sins of the whole world. Then he pierces it with the spear, remembering the words of the Gospel: "One of the soldiers pierced His side and straightway there came out blood and water." With the last words, he pours wine and water into the chalice. Out of the second loaf of holy bread the priest takes a small particle in honor and memory of the Mother of God and lays it on the paten at the right of the Lamb; this loaf is called "the Mother of God's." Out of the third loaf he takes nine particles, in honor of the various hosts of saints, who have been found worthy of habitation in Heaven, with the nine orders of angels, wherefore, this loaf is called "the Prósphora of the Nine Orders." The particles taken out of it are placed in three rows at the left of the Lamb. Out of the fourth loaf, called "the Prósphora of Health," particles are taken with a prayer for the health of living members of the Church and are laid below the Lamb. While lower still, under the "health particles," are placed those taken out of the fifth loaf, which is called "the Requiem-Prósphora," with a prayer for the dead.

Having laid the particles on the paten, the priest covers them with the asterisk, so as to keep them in the order in which they were laid, and, in doing so, remembers the star which stopped over the house in Bethlehem, wherein the Infant Jesus dwelt. Then the priest covers the paten and the chalice with the veils and the aër in token that Christ, from the first moment of His coming into the world, clothed Himself with glory, that His glory covers the whole world, and that He covers us also with His grace.

Thus, the rites of the Proskomedia commemorate the Nativity of Jesus Christ, Who, from the first moment of His incarnation, was the Lamb destined to be sacrificed for the sins of men, and, at the same time the King, Who gathered the believing around Himself as subjects. We are reminded that, notwithstanding His seeming humiliation, the Divine glory covered Him and shone forth as a star.

Having prepared the elements of the Sacrament, the priest prays, swinging the censer, that the Lord may bless the gifts (elements) and accept them, in memory of those who offered them and of those on whose behalf they were offered, and that He may keep him, the priest, worthy to celebrate the Holy Mystery.

2. The Liturgy of the Catechumens

Meaning of the Liturgy of the Catechumens, Its Component Parts and Its Beginning

The second part of the Liturgy is named "the Liturgy of the Catechumens," because, not only the faithful may be present at it, i.e., those who have received baptism, but also the catechumens, who are preparing for baptism, and the penitents, i.e., such Christians as are, for their sins, excluded from holy communion for a time. This part of the Liturgy consists only of prayers, hymns in honor of the Most Holy Trinity, and readings from the Word of God.

It begins with a glorification of the Kingdom of the Most Holy Trinity, that Kingdom of truth and peace which Jesus came to establish on earth. Then the Great Ectenia, or Ectenia of Peace, is recited, in which we pray that the Lord may give us His peace from above, without which the Kingdom of Heaven may not be entered, and "pacify" the lives of all men on earth.

The Typical Psalms and the Antiphons

Having besought the mercy of the Lord, we sing hymns regarding the greatest of all His mercies—the Incarnation of the Son of God. These hymns are sung alternately by two choirs, whence they are called Antiphons. They are divided by two Small Ecteniæ into three parts, in honor of the Most Holy Trinity. To the second Antiphon is always added a hymn in honor of the Incarnate Son of God: "O Only-begotten Son and Word of God, Who art immortal, yet didst deign for our salvation to be incarnate of the Holy Theotokos and Ever-Virgin Mary, and without change didst become man [became man without ceasing to be God], and wast crucified, O Christ God, trampling down death by death, Thou Who art one of the Holy Trinity [one of the persons of the Holy Trinity], glorified with the Father and the Holy Spirit, save us."

Antiphons are of various kinds. On Sundays and feast-days, Psalms 102 and 145 are sung. They are called "Typical Antiphons," because they are typical of the mercy of God to man.

> *Verses from Psalm 102 (The First Antiphon):* "Bless the Lord, O my soul, and all that is within me bless His holy name. Bless the Lord, O my soul, and forget not that He hath done for thee, Who is gracious unto all thine iniquities, Who healeth all thine infirmities, Who redeemeth thy life from corruption, Who crowneth thee with mercy and compassion, Who fulfilleth thy desire with good things, Compassionate and merciful is the Lord, longsuffering and plenteous in mercy. . . ."
>
> *Verses from Psalm 145 (Second Antiphon):* "Praise the Lord, O my soul. I will praise the Lord in my life, I will chant unto my God for as long I have my being. . . ."[26]

When these Psalms are sung, the Beatitudes take the place of the third Antiphon. This is the name given to Christ's sayings about them that are blessed, combined with the troparia of the daily or feast-day canon. On great feast-days the Antiphons consist of prophetic verses selected from Psalms appropriate to the festive event, and to them are joined hymns indicating the nature of the feast.

THE ENTRY WITH THE GOSPEL

Immediately after the hymns in honor of the Holy Trinity, the faithful are prepared for the lessons from the Scriptures. In the old times of persecution, the holy Book was brought out of the repository for the sacred vessels, which was in a secret place. This custom has been preserved as a memorial of the old usage, and as an allusion to Christ's coming and bringing the preaching of the Gospel into the world. The deacon opens the royal gates and brings out, through the northern door, the Gospel which lies on the altar, preceded by a candle-bearer and followed by the priest. The lighted candle indicates that the Word of God is light to our spirit, that the Law of God consecrates the path of our life, and that we are expected to harbor the light of faith and the warmth of love, without which the teaching of Christ would be as unintelligible to us as is the instruction of parents to children who do not love them or believe in them. Standing before the royal gates, the priest gives a blessing towards the East, with the words: "Blessed is the entry of Thy Saints, O Lord"; then the deacon calls out: "Wisdom. Aright!," alluding to the wisdom which is contained in the meaning of this entry, and inviting reverent attention. On great feast-days,[27] this is followed by a short verse from the Psalms containing a prophecy concerning the commemorated event. In the Book of the Gospel the faithful see Christ Himself, Who came into the world to preach His doctrine, and adore Him by singing the solemn hymn: "O come, let us worship, and fall down before Christ; O Son of God, Who didst rise from the dead, save us, who sing to Thee: Alleluia, alleluia, alleluia!" Then are sung the troparion and the kontakion for the day or feast, in which are pictured the mercies bestowed on us by the coming of the Saviour.

The Trisagion ("Thrice-Holy")

The priest concludes the troparion and the kontakion by the exclamation: "For holy art Thou, our God, and unto Thee do we send up glory," thus inviting the worshippers to celebrate the Holy Trinity to which the worshippers respond by singing the Trisagion: "Holy God, Holy Mighty, Holy Immortal One, have mercy on us." When the celebrant is assisted by a deacon, the Trisagion is brought out with greater emphasis. After the kontakion, the deacon asks a blessing of the priest: "Bless, Master, the time of the Trisagion," and having received the blessing at the exclamation, "For holy art Thou, our God," turns round and faces the people, saying "O Lord, save the pious and hearken unto us." The choir repeats this petition, then chants the Trisagion.

On the days of the Nativity of Christ, of the Epiphany, on Lazarus' Saturday and on Holy Saturday, during the Paschal week and on the day of Pentecost, the following words are sung instead of the Trisagion: "As many as have been baptized into Christ have put on Christ. Alleluia." The reason for this substitution is that in ancient times, catechumens were wont to receive the sacrament of baptism preferably on those days. The Church has preserved the custom in order that we, who have received baptism, may be mindful of the pledges we then gave. On the day of the Exaltation of the Cross (14th of September), and on the third Sunday in Lent, consecrated to the adoration of the Cross, the following is sung in place of the Trisagion: "Before Thy Cross, we bow down, O Master, and Thy holy Resurrection we glorify."

THE READINGS FROM THE APOSTLE AND THE GOSPEL

After the singing of the Trisagion, the celebrants retire to the Bema. A bishop stands on the Bema itself, a priest behind the altar next to the Bema. At the same time, the reader comes out into the middle of the Church bearing the Apostle and recites a prokimenon. In order to call the hearers' attention to it, as being a verse which indicates the substance of the lesson, the deacon exclaims, "Let us attend," after which the priest blesses the people, wishing them peace, and the deacon exclaims, "Wisdom!" After the prokimenon, the reader announces out of what book he is going to read, and the deacon once more invites attention, exclaiming, "Let us attend." Then begins the reading of the lesson for the day.

The reading of the Apostle is followed by that of the Gospel, i.e., of the lesson for the day out of one of the four evangelists. The worshippers are prepared also for the attentive hearing of the Gospel lesson. First, "Alleluia" is solemnly chanted, it having the same signification as the prokimenon before the Apostle. Only on Holy Saturday the following prokimenon is substituted for the "Alleluia:" "Arise, O God, judge the earth, for Thou shalt have an inheritance among all the nations." During the chanting of the "Alleluia," the censer is swung in allusion to the grace of God vouchsafed through His Word. Then the priest exclaims,

"Wisdom! Aright! Let us hear the holy Gospel," and blesses the people, wishing them peace, and the deacon announces from which Evangelist the lesson is taken. The worshippers give expression to their heartfelt joy by chanting, "Glory to Thee, our God, glory to Thee." The priest repeats his invitation, "Let us attend," and the deacon reads the Gospel lesson. After which, "Glory to Thee, our God, glory to Thee," is sung again, and the royal gates are closed.

COMMON PRAYERS FOR THE MEMBERS OF THE CHURCH AND DEPARTURE OF THE CATECHUMENS

After hearing the word of Christ Saviour, all present offer up prayers for all the members of the Church, living or dead, in the words of the Triple Ectenia. If, in the first part of the Liturgy, oblations were offered in memory of the dead, a special Requiem Ectenia is then recited. If the service includes prayers for deliverance from national disasters, such as an epidemic, famine, war, or for the deliverance of some particular Christian from sickness, from accidents while traveling, and the like, these petitions are added to those of the Triple Ectenia. These common prayers are followed by the special ectenia for the catechumens, in which we pray that the Lord may "teach them the Word of Truth, reveal to them the Gospel of Righteousness, unite them to His Church; that He may save them, have mercy on them, help them and keep them by His grace, so that they also with us may glorify His most honorable and majestic Name."

Immediately after these prayers follows the departure of the catechumens. The deacon repeatedly exclaims, "As many as are catechumens, depart." In ancient times the prayers of the faithful began only after the deacons had ascertained that none of the catechumens remained in the church. At the present time, when baptism is usually administered in infancy, there seldom are any catechumens in a church; consequently, the "departure of the catechumens" takes place rarely and not everywhere. But the allusion is preserved in the service, to remind the faithful of the vows they took at baptism, and arouse in them a humble consciousness of sin.

3. The Liturgy of the Faithful

WHAT THE LITURGY OF THE FAITHFUL REPRESENTS, AND THE PRINCIPAL ACTS WHICH COMPOSE IT

The third part of the Liturgy is named "The Liturgy of the Faithful," because none but the faithful—i.e., such persons as have received the Sacrament of Baptism and endeavor to live in accordance with the Christian—law may be present at the celebration thereof.

After the catechumens have left the church, the deacon calls out, "As many as are of the Faithful, again and again, in peace let us pray to the Lord," and with this invitation to prayer opens the Liturgy of the Faithful, in the course of which Christians call to mind the passion, death, burial, resurrection, ascension and second coming of Christ the Saviour, and pray that the Lord may accept their gifts and make them partakers in His Mystical Supper. The order of the prayers and rites of the Liturgy is disposed to correspond with these memories and petitions.

The Liturgy of the Faithful is divided into four parts: (a) the final preparation of the Elements and the faithful for the Sacrifice; (b) the offering of the Sacrifice, i.e., the performance of the Sacrament and commemoration of the members of the Church; (c) the preparation for Communion and the partaking of Communion; and (d) thanksgiving for Communion and the conclusion of the service.

(A.) Preparation of the Elements and the Faithful for the Sacrifice

THE GREAT ENTRY

After the two Small Ecteniæ for the faithful have been recited, ending with the exclamation, "Wisdom!," the royal gates are opened and the choir sings the hymn on the transfer of the Elements to the altar, which hymn is called the Cherubic Hymn, because we are preparing to minister at the Throne of God on earth even as the Cherubim minister at the Heavenly Throne.

The Cherubic Hymn

> Let us who mystically represent the Cherubim and chant the thrice-holy hymn unto the life-creating Trinity, now lay aside all earthly care. That we may receive the King of all, Who cometh invisibly upborne by the ranks of angels. Alleluia, alleluia, alleluia.[28]

While the Cherubic Hymn is sung, after censing with incense, the solemn transfer of the Elements from the table of oblations to the altar takes place. In the middle of the hymn, immediately after the words, "lay aside all earthly care," the singing is interrupted; at this moment the celebrants—the deacon holding the paten poised on his head, the priest holding the chalice in his hands, both preceded by candle bearers—come out of the northern door, and, stopping before the royal gates, with their faces to the people, pray first for the Russian Church (or other national Church), the local bishop and all Orthodox Christians,[29] "that the Lord may remember them in His Kingdom." When mentioning the members of the Church, the celebrants also mention on whose behalf and with what petitions the Sacrifice is to be offered. Then, entering the sanctuary by the royal gates, the priest places the paten and the chalice upon the unfolded Antimins, while the deacon closes the Royal Gates and draws the curtain behind it, in memory of the burial of Christ, Who received death for our sins. During this time the choir ends the Cherubic Hymn.

Christians reverently receive the Elements brought out to them, vividly recalling Christ as He, of His own free will, goeth forth to suffering and death, and pray, in the words of the penitent thief, "that He may remember them all also in His Kingdom."[30]

PETITION FOR SPIRITUAL MERCIES, EXHORTATION TO LOVE AND PEACE, AND PROFESSION OF FAITH

After the Cherubic Hymn follows the Ectenia of Supplication, in which, putting away all worldly care, we ask for spiritual mercies only. To the petitions of this ectenia is added a petition, "for the precious Gifts that have been offered."

After the ectenia the faithful are reminded of the things which are demanded of each of them in order that the Sacrifice which they offer may be acceptable to God: spiritual peace, mutual love, and unity of faith. The priest as he blesses the people, says "Peace be unto all," to which they reply, "And to thy spirit." Then the deacon exclaims "Let us love one another that with one mind we may confess"[31] — when the choir in the name of all present announces Who is to be confessed: "the Father and the Son and the Holy Spirit, the Trinity one in essence and indivisible." After which, they chant the profession of faith, the Creed or "Symbol of Faith."—"I believe in one God, the Father Almighty..." As faith reveals to us the mysteries of the Deity and proclaims the resurrection of Christ, Who accepted death on the Cross for our sake, the curtain is drawn away at this moment (as the seal from the grave), the veil is lifted from the Elements, and the priest fans them with it from above, symbolizing the breath of the grace of the Holy Spirit. In the East, this act of fanning the Elements was originally instituted and is maintained to this day, as a protection against dust and insects. In ancient times, the Christians did not reveal the mysteries of their faith to pagans and Jews; therefore, before the chanting of the Creed, the deacon called to the doorkeepers, "The doors! the doors!," ordering them to look out sharply that no unbaptized intruder might enter, then turned to those present, with the words, "In wisdom let us attend." At the present time, when there is no need of guarding the church doors, these words are uttered by the deacon as a reminder to the worshippers that they should guard the doors of their souls, and not admit into it any thoughts, wishes or feelings unworthy of the holiness of the great Sacrament.

INVITATION TO ATTEND

When the worshippers have ended their profession of faith, which entitles them to be present at the Liturgy of the Faithful, the deacon invites their reverent attention, so they may worthily offer the sacrifice to the Lord: "Let us stand well; let us stand with fear; let us attend, that we may offer the holy oblation in peace." The choir responds for the faithful, telling in what their sacrifice shall consist: "A mercy of peace (of spirit), a sacrifice of praise." Then the priest blesses their intention, saying: "The grace of our Lord Jesus Christ and the love of God the Father and the Communion of the Holy Spirit be with you all." The faithful receive this blessing with bowed heads, in token of reverence, and respond, "And with thy spirit." The priest once more invites the faithful to attend closely and to keep free of all earthly things: "Let us lift up our hearts!" to which the faithful respond, "We lift them up unto the Lord." With this ends the preparation for the Sacrament of the Eucharist.

(B.) The Fulfillment of the Sacrament

THE PRAYER OF THANKSGIVING, THE OFFERING, AND CONSECRATION OF THE GIFTS

The consummation of the Sacrament begins with the priest's exclamation: "Let us give thanks unto the Lord." The faithful, in response to this invitation, worship the Lord, and, mindful of all His mercies, sing the hymn: "It is meet and right to worship the Father, and the Son, and the Holy Spirit, the Trinity one in essence and indivisible." In order that the absent also may, at this solemn instant of the service, join their prayers of thanksgiving to those of the faithful in the church, the bells are set tolling (in single-strokes). After worshipping the Holy Trinity, the priest lifts the asterisk from the paten, and invites the people to express their thanksgiving to the Lord not only by worship but also by singing the triumphal hymn in His honor: "Singing, shouting, crying aloud, and saying:" (i.e., "let us give thanks to the Lord, singing a triumphal hymn to Him with all the powers of our souls"[32]) and the faithful, in, response to this invitation, sing the triumphal hymn composed of the song of the Angels who surround the Throne Of God in heaven, and that with which the Jews met Christ on the occasion of His festive entrance into Jerusalem: "Holy, holy, holy Lord of Sabaoth (Lord of hosts), Heaven and earth are filled with Thy glory! —Hosanna in the highest! —Blessed is He that cometh in the name of the Lord! Hosanna in the highest!"[33]

Having rendered thanks to God for all His mercies by worship and songs of praise, the priest utters the words in which Christ instituted the Sacrament of the Eucharist, which is the greatest monument of God's supreme love for men: "Take, eat (the bread); this is My Body which is broken for you for the remission of sins"; and "drink ye of it, all of you (the cup); this is My Blood of the New Testament,[34] which is shed for you and for many, for the remission of sins." The faithful, calling to mind at these words the Mystical Supper, the passion and death of Christ, respond, "Amen."

Then the priest, in fulfillment of Christ's command, to "do this in memory of Him," raises the paten and the chalice, saying as he does so: "Thine own, of Thine own we offer unto Thee in behalf of all and for all" (i.e., "What is Thine own we offer, from Thine own servants in behalf of all men, and for all Thy mercies"); and the faithful, taking up his words, chant: "We praise Thee, we bless Thee, We give thanks unto Thee, O Lord, and we pray unto Thee, our God." While this hymn is being chanted the priest prays that the Lord may send down His Holy Spirit on the offered Gifts, consecrate them, and change the bread into His true Body, and the wine into His true Blood, then blesses the Gifts. At this instant, by the might of God, the bread and the wine are changed in substance into the Body and Blood of Christ. All who are present in the Church express their veneration for the sacred Mystery by a prostration.

COMMEMORATING THE MEMBERS OF THE CHURCH

After the consecration of the elements, the priest commemorates the members of the Church, in whose behalf they have been offered. He says in his prayer that we offer this sacrifice for all the Saints who have gone to their rest (i.e., died)—more especially for the Mother of God —and that we beseech Him that, hearing their prayers, He may visit us and be mindful of all those who have died in the hope of a resurrection. The deacon at the same time reads the Diptychs—the lists of names of deceased Christians. After praying for the dead, the priest prays for the living — that the Lord may be mindful of the bishops, the priests, and of all Christian people. This commemoration of the members of the Church the priest begins while the choir is singing, "We praise Thee." When this prayer is ended, he commemorates aloud the Mother of God: "Especially for our most holy, most pure, most blessed, glorious Lady Theotokos and Ever-Virgin Mary." To this prayer the faithful respond with a hymn of praise in honor of the Mother of God, "It is truly meet to bless thee." On great feast days, the choir sings in the place of this hymn the eirmos of the ninth ode of the matins canon. While the hymn "It is truly meet" is being sung, the priest proceeds with the commemoration of the members of the church and when it is ended, he commemorates aloud from among the living, the bishops, as the governors and pastors of the Church: "Among the first, remember, O Lord, the Orthodox episcopate of the Church of Russia" (or another national Church); "and our lord the Very Most Reverend Metropolitan N., First Hierarch of the Russian Church Abroad; and our lord, the Most Reverend (Archbishop or Bishop, N., *whose diocese it is*), whom do Thou grant unto Thy holy churches in peace, safety, honor, health, and length of days rightly dividing the Word of Thy truth."[35] The deacon during this time reads the list of the living who are to be commemorated.

The priest ends the commemoration of the members of the Church with the prayer: "And grant unto us (i.e., help us—all that have been commemorated together with the Saints and all who have died in the hope of resurrection) that with one mouth and one heart we may glorify and hymn Thy most honorable and majestic Name, of the Father and of the Son and of the Holy Spirit, now, and ever and unto the ages of ages." The worshippers respond, "Amen!" in token of their participation in the offering of the Sacrifice and in the commemoration of the members of the Church. This part of the Liturgy of the Faithful also concludes with the priest's blessing: "And may the mercies of our great God and of our Saviour Jesus Christ be with you all," and with the worshippers wishing the priest the same mercies: "And with thy spirit."

(C.) The Preparation for Communion and the Act of Communion

THE PREPARATION OF THE FAITHFUL FOR COMMUNION

Immediately after the commemoration of all the members of the Church, begins the preparation of the faithful for Communion. The deacon recites the Ectenia of Supplication, which he begins with the invitation: "Having called to remembrance all the Saints, again and again in peace let us pray to the Lord," to which he adds a petition for the precious Gifts offered and consecrated, that the Lord, accepting them at His holy, heavenly and spiritual altar (i.e., non-substantial not like the material altar erected by us), as the odor of a spiritual sweet smell, may in return send down upon us the divine grace and the gift of the Holy Spirit and deliver us from all affliction, wrath and necessity. The ectenia concludes with the priest's praying that the Lord may vouchsafe to let us address Him uncondemned as our Father, in the Lord's Prayer: "And vouchsafe us, O Master, that with boldness, and without condemnation, we may dare to call upon Thee, the Heavenly God as Father, and to say, "Our Father, Who art in the Heavens," etc. The Lord's Prayer is then chanted by the faithful (the choir). Then the priest gives them his blessing with the good wish, "Peace be unto all," and the deacon invites them to bow down their heads before the Lord. At this moment the curtain is drawn; the priest, after the deacon's exclamation, "Let us attend," elevates the consecrated Lamb, saying: "Holy things are for the holy!" (i.e., the holy gifts can be offered only to those who are holy.) All present, with profound veneration, worship with a prostration the Holy Lamb, and say in the consciousness of their unworthiness: "One is holy, One is Lord, Jesus Christ, to the glory of God the Father. Amen."

The Preparation of the Gifts for Communion and the Communion of the Celebrants

After the faithful have been prepared for receiving holy communion, the priest breaks the Lamb in four parts, saying: "Broken and distributed is the Lamb of God: broken, yet not divided; ever eaten, though never consumed, but sanctifying them that partake thereof," —and places these parts on the paten in the shape of a Cross. Then he places one portion in the chalice with the words: "The fullness of the Holy Spirit," (meaning that the Sacrament is fulfilled through the action of the Holy Spirit), then he blesses the warm water, saying: "Blessed is the warmth (i.e., the warmth of heart) of Thy Saints," and pours some into the chalice, saying: "The warmth of faith is full of the Holy Spirit" (i.e., the warmth of faith is enkindled in the human soul through the action of the Holy Spirit). Uniting the Body and Blood of Christ, the priest remembers the resurrection of Christ from the dead, and, by the words uttered at that moment, indicates that the Sacrament is fulfilled through the action of the Holy Spirit, that only one possessed of warm faith may participate in this Sacrament, and that this faith is enkindled in the human soul by the grace of the Holy Spirit.

After all these acts have been performed, the celebrants take communion, partaking first of the Body, then of the Blood of Christ, after which the remaining portions of the Lamb are placed into the chalice, the Sunday hymns being recited the while. If there are no communicants (i.e., no persons duly prepared to receive holy communion), all the portions taken out of the oblation-loaves in honor of the Virgin and the Saints and in memory of the dead and the living are now placed into the chalice, with the prayer, "Cleanse, O Lord, the sins of those here commemorated, by Thy precious Blood and by the prayers of Thy Saints." If there are communicants, these portions remain in the paten until after the communion of the faithful.

During the act of breaking the Lamb, of uniting the Elements, and of communion by the celebrants, a hymn is sung, which is called "the Communion Hymn," and which relates to the memories of the day and the lessons from the Gospels and the Apostle. The communion hymn for Sunday is, "Praise the Lord from the Heavens, praise Him in the highest. Amen." This hymn is usually followed by the sermon or homily.

THE COMMUNION OF LAYMEN

After the communion hymn and the homily, the curtain is drawn away, the royal gates are opened; the deacon brings out the chalice with the Sacrament, stands on the ambo, and calls out: "With the fear of God, and with faith draw near!" The faithful venerate the Sacrament with a prostration, remembering Christ who rose from the dead and appeared to His disciples after His resurrection, and sing: "Blessed is He that cometh in the name of the Lord; God is the Lord, and hath appeared unto us." Then the communicants approach the ambo, make their profession of faith in the Sacrament of the Eucharist, and beseech the Lord that He may admit them to participate in His Mystical Supper and vouchsafe to let them receive His holy communion uncondemned.

Prayers before Communion

I believe, O Lord, and I confess that Thou art truly the Christ, the Son of the living God, Who didst come into the world to save sinners of whom I am chief. Moreover, I believe that this is truly Thy most pure Body, and that this is truly Thine own precious Blood. Wherefore, I pray Thee: have mercy on me and forgive me my transgressions, voluntary and involuntary, in word and deed, in knowledge and in ignorance. And vouchsafe me to partake without condemnation of Thy most pure Mysteries unto the remission of sins and life everlasting. Amen. — Of Thy Mystical Supper, O Son of God, receive me today as a communicant; for I will not speak of the Mystery to Thine enemies, nor will I give Thee a kiss as did Judas, but like the Thief do I confess Thee: Remember me, O Lord, in Thy kingdom. Let not the communion of Thy holy Mysteries be unto me for judgment or condemnation, O Lord, but for healing of soul and body.[36]

Then, after a prostration, the communicants, one by one, without crowding one another, and with hands reverently crossed on the breast, approach the chalice, receive the Body and Blood of Christ out of the spoon from the hands of the priest, and very gently kiss the edge of the chalice, as it were the side of Christ Himself. As he gives the communion to each, the priest says: "The servant (or handmaid) of God, N., partaketh of the precious and holy Body and Blood of our Lord and God and Saviour, Jesus Christ, unto the remission of sins and life everlasting." The communicant retires and makes a reverent obeisance, but not a prostration; for, having become mystically united to Christ, he is now a child of God, and the prostration is a sign of servitude. During the time that laymen receive communion, the choir repeatedly sings: "Receive ye the Body of Christ, taste ye of the fountain of immortality. Alleluia!" Having administered the Sacrament to all the communicants, the priest carries the chalice to the altar and places in it the portions taken out of the oblation-breads on behalf of the living and the dead.

THE BLESSING AND THE LAST APPEARANCE OF THE HOLY GIFTS BEFORE THE PEOPLE

This part of the Liturgy ends, like the preceding ones, with a blessing. Having placed the chalice upon the altar, the priest steps out of the sanctuary and, standing on the ambo, blesses the people, speaking this prayer: "Save, O God, Thy people, and bless Thine inheritance." In answer to this, the choir sings a hymn which sets forth what mercies the people have received through Christ: "We have seen the true Light, we have received the Heavenly Spirit, we have found the True Faith. We worship the indivisible Trinity, for He hath saved us." While this hymn is being sung, the priest censes the chalice, which holds the holy Gifts and when it is ended, the deacon carries the paten to the altar, and the priest, taking up the chalice, faces the people and utters the concluding words of the Doxology: "Always, now and ever, and unto the ages of ages." The faithful make an obeisance to the very ground, remembering the ascension of Christ to Heaven.

(D.) Conclusion of the Service

Giving Thanks for Communion

Having adored Christ manifested for the last time in His holy Sacrament, the Christians sing the hymn of thanksgiving: "Let our mouth be filled with Thy praise, O Lord, that we may hymn Thy glory, for Thou hast vouchsafed us to partake of Thy holy, divine, immortal and life-giving Mysteries; keep us in Thy holiness, that we may meditate on Thy righteousness all the day long. Alleluia." (i.e., help us to preserve in ourselves the holiness which we have received through communion, that we may through this whole day study to live righteously, according to Thy word.) The deacon also gives thanks in the prayers of the Small Ectenia, which differs from the ordinary one in that instead of beginning with the words, "Again and again," etc., it begins as follows: "Aright! Having partaken of the divine, holy, most pure, immortal, heavenly and life-giving fearful Mysteries of Christ, let us worthily give thanks unto the Lord."

BLESSING FOR GOING FORTH OUT OF THE CHURCH; PRAYER RECITED BEFORE THE AMBO; DISTRIBUTION OF HOLY BREAD OR *ANTIDORON*; AND DISMISSAL

After thanks have been given, the priest blesses the Christians who are to go forth out of the church, reminding them that they should go forth and live outside of it in the same peace with which they entered it. "In peace let us depart," he says. To this the choir responds, speaking for all, "In the name of the Lord." Then the priest, stepping down from the ambo, and standing in the midst of the people, recites a prayer which is an epitome of the entire service. He prays that the Lord may save His people and bless His inheritance, the fullness of His Church (i.e., the entire Christian community), that He may preserve and sanctify those who love the splendor of His house; that He may not forsake us, who hope in Him, and that He may grant peace to the whole world, to His churches, to the priesthood, and to all His people." The choir, speaking for all, express the wish to go forth with the blessing of God: "Blessed be the Name of the Lord from henceforth and for evermore," is sung thrice, after which Psalm 33 is sung: "I will bless the Lord at all times."

During the singing of the Psalm, the priest distributes pieces of holy bread. These are the remnants of the oblation-loaf out of which a portion —the Lamb—has been cut in memory of Christ, and is called *Antidóron*, which means, "Substitute for the Gift." The Antidoron is distributed in order that those who have not received communion may also, at least in thought, share in the Sacrament of the Eucharist, that they may not feel left out of the community of the faithful, but be in communion with them. The distribution of the Antidoron is a survival of the *agápes* or love-feasts which, among the early Christians, were made up of the remains of the offerings brought.

After the reading of the Psalm, and the distribution of the Antidoron, the priest blesses the people in the name of the Lord, saying, "The blessing of the Lord be upon you, by His grace and love for mankind." The service ends with a prayerful wish that the Lord may have mercy on us through the intercession of the Mother of God, and of His Saints, and that He may give us length of days.

The communicants remain after the dismissal, to listen to more prayers of thanksgiving for communion.

DAYS WHEN THE LITURGY OF ST. BASIL THE GREAT IS PERFORMED, AND WHEREIN IT DIFFERS FROM THAT OF ST. JOHN CHRYSOSTOM

The Liturgy as ordered by St. Basil the Great, Archbishop of Cæsarea in Cappadocia, is performed only ten times in the year: on the Vigils of Christmas and Epiphany (if these vigils do not fall on a Saturday or Sunday, in which case the Liturgy of St. Basil the Great is performed on the feast-day itself, and that of St. John Chrysostom on the vigil); on the first of January, that being the day dedicated to the memory of St. Basil; on the Sundays of Lent, with the exception of Palm Sunday; on Thursday and Saturday of the Holy Week.

The Liturgy of Basil the Great differs from that of John Chrysostom only in the following points: (1) the secret prayers, which the priest recites inaudibly while performing the sacrifice are longer, and, therefore, the hymns which accompany the act are sung to a slower time; (2) the words of the institution of the Sacrament are given as follows "He gave to His holy disciples and apostles and said: take and eat..." and "He gave to His holy disciples and apostles and said: take and drink..."; (3) in the place of the hymn "It is truly meet," the hymn sung is: "In thee rejoiceth, thou who art full of grace, all creation"; (4) in the dismissal prayer, the name of Basil the Great is mentioned instead of John Chrysostom's.

THE TYPICA

When on days on which the church statutes prescribe that the Liturgy shall be celebrated, but it is not possible to do so, either from the lack of a church or because the priest has failed to prepare himself for partaking of the Sacrament, the Rite of the Typica is substituted for the Liturgy. This service begins with the singing, immediately after the Great Ectenia, of the two Psalms, 102 ("Bless the Lord, O my Soul, and all that is within me bless His holy name"), and 145 ("Praise the Lord, O my Soul"), which, in the complete Liturgy, are used as Typical Antiphons. These Psalms are followed by the hymn "O only-begotten Son...," which contains the Christian doctrine of the Incarnation, and by the Beatitudes, with the penitent thief's prayer, "Remember me, O Lord, in Thy Kingdom," repeated between the verses. After the Beatitudes, the Apostle and the Gospel are read, the Triple Ectenia is recited, the Creed is chanted, followed by the Ectenia of Supplication, and, in conclusion, the Lord's Prayer and Dismissal.

Special Features of Divine Service On Feast-Days and In Fast-Times

Immovable Feasts and Fasts

The Nativity of the Most Holy Theotokos

The Most Holy Virgin Mary was born in the Galilean town of Nazareth. Her parents were Saints Joachim and Anna. St. Joachim came from the tribe of Judah, from the royal house of David, while St. Anna was of the tribe of Levi, from the high-priestly house of Aaron. For a long time they had no children, which caused them much grief, and they entreated God that He would take away the dishonor of childlessness. The Lord heard their prayer and granted them a daughter, whom they named Mary, which means "lady" or "lofty." This event which was so joyous for the human race since it opened the door to salvation, is celebrated September 8th. The following day is dedicated to the memory of Joachim and Anna, who are called "Ancestors of God," since their daughter Mary was deemed worthy to be the mother of the God-man, Jesus Christ.

Troparion of the Feast

Thy nativity, O Theotokos Virgin, hath proclaimed joy to all the world; for from thee hath dawned the Son of Righteousness, Christ our God, annulling the curse and bestowing the blessing, abolishing death and granting us life eternal.[37]

The Universal Feast of the Exaltation of the Precious and Life-Giving Cross of the Lord

The feast of the Exaltation of the Cross is celebrated on the 14th of September, in memory of two events: (1) the finding by the Empress Helena, mother of the Emperor Constantine the Great, of the precious Cross on which Christ Saviour was crucified; and (2) the restoration of this same Cross from captivity with the Persians by the Greek Emperor Heraclius. The feast is named the *Exaltation* because, when the Cross of Christ was found, it was elevated, "exalted," that all might see it and *Universal* because the Christians, in their joy at the return of the Cross from captivity, resolved that this event should be celebrated all over the world.

As the finding and exalting of the Cross of Christ was a triumph of the Christian faith, which the Emperors had declared the dominant religion of the Empire, the hymns for the day contain principally prayers for the pious Emperor and for the Christian people. This character is expressed in the troparion for the day: "Save, O Lord, Thy people and bless Thine inheritance, granting our pious Emperor victories over his opponents and preserving the community by Thy Cross." When there is no Christian Empire, we sing instead: "Save, O Lord, Thy people and bless Thine inheritance, grant Thou unto Orthodox Christians victory over enemies, and by the power of Thy Cross do Thou preserve Thy commonwealth."

The chief peculiarity of the service is that, on the vigil of the feast, after Vespers, the Cross is brought out of the repository of sacred vessels, as though out of the depths of the earth, and is placed upon the altar. Then at Matins, after the Great Doxology, to the slow singing of the Trisagion, it is brought out of the Sanctuary and placed on a specially decorated lectern, for public veneration. For this ceremony the priest dons all the vestments of his order; he carries the Cross on his head, on a platter, coming through the northern door, in token that Christ, although invested with divine glory, came into the world in humiliation. All Christians, the celebrants first, then the laymen, approach the Cross, venerate it with two prostrations, then kiss it and perform one more prostration. During all this time the choir sings the hymn: "Before Thy Cross we fall down, O Master, and Thy holy Resurrection we glorify." In order that those absent from the church may, mentally at least, share in the veneration of the Cross, the church bells ring a carillon during the ceremony. The Cross remains on the lectern until the 21st of September, when, after the Liturgy and dismissal, it is solemnly taken up and carried into the Sanctuary through the royal gates. The celebration of this feast is accompanied by strict fasting, in memory of the Passion of Christ, and as a token that the Christian should follow after Christ by the road of suffering, by mortifying his passions and carnal desires.

In great churches and in monasteries, the veneration is preceded by the ceremony of exalting the Cross. The priest, having brought out the Cross, places it on the lectern, censes it, then, taking it up in his hands, stands with his face turned towards the East (towards the Sanctuary). During this time the deacon recites an ectenia consisting of five petitions; after each petition the "Lord have mercy on us" is chanted a hundred times. During the chanting of each hundred, the rite of exaltation is performed: the priest elevates the Cross, first towards the East, then towards the West, South and North, then once more towards the East. At the beginning of each hundred, he makes the sign of the Cross thrice in the direction in which he performs the exaltation; then, holding the Cross in his hands, he slowly bows his head nearly to the ground, then raises it as slowly; towards the end of the hundred he stands upright and blesses the people with the Cross thrice. After the exaltation, the veneration of the Cross takes place.

The Entry of the Most Holy Theotokos into the Temple

Righteous Joachim and Anna, even before the birth of their daughter Mary, had vowed to dedicate to God the child whom He would grant them. When the Most Holy Virgin Mary was still a young girl, they brought her into the Temple, accompanied by virgins with lamps, and they placed her on the first step of the stairway. According to ancient tradition, Mary ascended the fifteen steps into the Temple by herself. At the top of the stairway the high priest met her and, full of the Holy Spirit, led her not only into the altar, but even into the Holy of Holies, where according to the Law, he himself was allowed to enter only once a year. The people were amazed at the entry, and the angels of God marveled as well. Christians celebrate this event on November 21st as a portent of the reconciliation of man to God through the power of Christ.

Troparion of the Feast

Today is the prelude of God's goodwill and the heralding of the salvation of mankind. In the temple of God, the Virgin is presented openly, and she proclaimeth Christ unto all. To her then with a great voice let us cry aloud: Rejoice, O thou fulfillment of the Creator's dispensation.[38]

The Nativity of Our Lord God and Saviour Jesus Christ

Of all the twelve great feast-days, that of the Nativity of Christ (25th of December), is celebrated with particular solemnity. For the worthy celebration of it, Christians prepare by a fast of forty days, called the Nativity Fast, which lasts from the 15th of November to the 24th of December inclusively. It is popularly known also as "Philip's Fast" because it begins the day after that consecrated to the memory of the Apostle Philip (14th of November). Already from the day of the Virgin's Entry into the Temple, hymns are sung in honor of the Nativity. Especially at Matins, odes from the Christmas canon are sung: "Christ is born, give ye glory; Christ comes from heaven, meet ye Him. Christ is on earth, be ye exalted. Sing unto the Lord all the earth, and in gladness sing praises, O ye people, for He is glorified." The two last Sundays before the Nativity are sacred to the memory of all the Old Testament Saints, who were saved by faith in the coming Saviour. The first of these Sundays is called, "the Sunday of the Ancient Fathers," and is consecrated to the memory of the holy Patriarchs, from Adam to Joseph, who was betrothed to Mary the Mother of God, and of the holy Prophets, from Samuel to John the Baptist; while the second is called, "the Sunday of the Holy Fathers," and is consecrated to the memory of Christ's forefathers in the flesh.

The vigil of this feast is observed by keeping a strict fast. The Church prescribes that on this day boiled wheat be the only food used, or boiled rice with raisins and honey *(Kutyá)*, irrespective of the day of the week. As to the services on this vigil, they differ according to the day of the week. If it falls on a Monday, Tuesday, Wednesday, Thursday or Friday: the so-called "Royal Hours" are read, then follow Vespers combined with the Liturgy of Basil the Great;[39] on Christmas Day itself the Liturgy of John Chrysostom is celebrated. If the vigil falls on a Saturday or on a Sunday, then: (1) the Royal Hours are read on Friday, and on that Friday there is no Liturgy; (2) on the vigil itself the Liturgy of Chrysostom is celebrated in the morning, then (3) Vespers with lessons from the Apostle and the Gospel after the Vespers entry; (4) on Christmas Day, the Liturgy of Basil the Great is celebrated.

"Royal Hours" differ from the ordinary in the following points: (1) of the three Psalms prescribed for each Hour, only one is read; the other two are selected specially with reference to the events commemorated; (2) at each Hour after the troparia, the paremiæ, the Apostle/Epistle and the Gospel are read; and (3) the offices of all the three Hours are combined into one. These Hours are called "Royal" because they are read only on the eve of the most important days of Christ's earthly life—on the vigils of the Nativity and the Epiphany and on Holy Friday; and also because in ancient times the Emperors used to go in solemn procession to the principal church of the city on these days.

The Liturgy or the Vespers service is followed by the "glorification of Christ:" a lighted candle is placed in the middle of the church, symbolizing the light of Christ, and the celebrants, standing before it, sing the troparion and the kontakion of the feast. This ceremony is afterwards performed in the homes of Christians desirous to bring the joy of Christmas into their own houses, their own families.

Troparion of the Nativity

Thy Nativity, O Christ our God, hath shined upon the world the light of knowledge; for thereby, they that worshipped the stars were taught by a Star to worship Thee, the Sun of Righteousness, and to know Thee, the Dayspring from on high. O Lord, glory be to Thee.

Kontakion of the Nativity

Today the Virgin giveth birth to Him Who is transcendent in essence, [Him Who was before all things]; and the earth offereth a cave to Him Who is unapproachable. Angels with shepherds give glory, with a star the Magi do journey, for our sake a young Child is born, Who is pre-eternal God.[40]

The All-night Vigil before the Nativity consists of the Great Compline and Matins. On the day of the feast itself, after the Liturgy, formerly a *moleben* of thanksgiving would be performed, for "the deliverance from the invasion of the Gauls and twenty nations with them," in the year 1812. This service would conclude with the proclamation of length of days to the Emperor, to his house and the Christ-loving army, and of "eternal remembrance" for the Emperor Alexander I.

On the day following the Nativity, the Most Holy Mother of God is celebrated, as the person who was the instrument of the Incarnation of the Son of God. On the Sunday following the Nativity are commemorated Joseph, the betrothed, King David, and James, the brother of the Lord. If this Sunday falls on the 1st of January, after the conclusion of the festivities of the Nativity, which is prescribed for the 31st of December, this commemoration is performed on the 26th of December.

In honor of the great festival, fasting is dispensed with on the Wednesdays and Fridays between the day of the Nativity and the vigil of the Epiphany, whence these two weeks are called "unbroken."

The Baptism of Our Lord God and Saviour Jesus Christ

The feast of the Baptism of our Lord, celebrated on the 6th day of January, is also called the *Theophany* or *Epiphany* (Divine Manifestation, Manifestation from Above), because at the baptism of Jesus Christ, the Trinity was present and manifested: the Son of God received baptism in the River Jordan; God the Father testified to His Son by a voice from Heaven; and the Holy Spirit, appearing in the form of a dove, confirmed the words of God the Father. In ancient times, catechumens used to receive the Sacrament of Baptism on the vigil of this day; hence, it also received the name of the *Feast of Illumination*.

Troparion of the Feast

When Thou wast baptized in the Jordan, O Lord, the worship of the Trinity was made manifest; for the voice of the Father bare witness unto Thee, calling Thee His beloved Son. And the Spirit in the form of a dove confirmed the certainty of His word. O Christ our God, Who hast appeared, and hast enlightened the world, glory be to Thee.

Kontakion of the Feast

Thou hast appeared today unto the whole world, and Thy light, O Lord, hath been signed upon us who with knowledge chant unto Thee: Thou hast come, Thou hast appeared, O Light Unapproachable.[41]

The services on this day are the same as on the day of the Nativity of Christ. The vigil is a day of strict fasting as that of the vigil of the Nativity;

and on the day following, the faithful congregate to celebrate the holy and glorious Prophet and Forerunner, John the Baptizer of Christ.[42]

The special feature of the service on the day of the Epiphany is "the Blessing of the Waters." In all churches it takes place on the Vigil of the feast, after the Liturgy or Vespers. In some churches, it is repeated on the day of the feast after the Liturgy, on rivers and lakes, whither the clergy go in procession, with Cross and banners. The first blessing is retained as a reminder of the baptism which catechumens used to receive on this day, and of the vows which we ourselves took at our own baptism. The second blessing takes place in memory of the Baptism of Our Lord; hence, the procession is called "going to Jordan." The service of blessing consists of the chanting of sticheræ, the reading of paremiaæ, of readings from the Apostle and the Gospels, prayers offered by the priest for the sanctification of the waters,[43] and in the thrice-repeated immersion of the Cross, to the chanting of the troparion of the feast. After the ceremony, the celebrants, as on the vigil of the Nativity, sing the troparion and the kontakion of the feast in the middle of the church, standing before the lighted candle. Then, carrying with them some of the blessed water, they go to the homes of their parishioners and sprinkle them with the water.

The Meeting of our Lord Jesus Christ

According to the Law of Moses, on the fortieth day after the birth of the first-born male child, the mother was obliged to present the boy to the Lord, that is, bring him into the Temple and offer sacrifice for her own cleansing and as a ransom for her first-born son. A sheep and a turtle dove were offered, but if the family was poor, only two doves or turtle doves. The ransom was set by the Law at five shekels. On the fortieth day after the birth of Jesus, the Most Holy Virgin Mary came to the Temple with her Child and offered the sacrifice of two doves. Christ was met in the Temple by the godly elder Symeon, to whom the Holy

Spirit had revealed that he would not die until he had seen the Christ. By divine revelation Symeon knew that the baby Jesus was the Saviour of the world. He took Him into his hands, thanked God, and called Jesus "a light unto the Gentiles and the glory of Israel." At that time there lived in the Temple the eighty-four year old widow and prophetess Anna. She approached Mary, glorified God, and spoke about Christ to all who were awaiting deliverance. This event is commemorated on February 2nd, and the following day is dedicated to the memory of Sts. Symeon the God-receiver and Anna the Prophetess.

Troparion of the Feast

Rejoice, thou who art full of grace, O Virgin Theotokos, for from thee hath risen the Sun of Righteousness, Christ our God, enlightening those in darkness. Rejoice thou also, O righteous Elder, as thou receivest in thine arms the Redeemer of our souls, Who also granteth unto us the Resurrection.[44]

The Annunciation

The feast of the Annunciation is celebrated on the 25th of March. On the day following, the faithful congregate to celebrate the Archangel Gabriel, who brought the joyful tidings to the Virgin Mary. This feast usually comes in Lent, sometimes on one of the first days of the Paschal week. But in spite of the Lenten time, it is celebrated so brightly as not to be darkened by the sad Lenten services of even the Holy Week. Nor is it lost in the radiance of the Paschal Week. Christians thus express the fact that they look on the Annunciation as on the beginning of our salvation.

Troparion of the Feast

Today is the fountainhead of our salvation and the manifestation of the mystery which was from eternity. The Son of God becometh the Virgin's Son, and Gabriel proclaimeth the good tidings of grace; wherefore, we also cry to the Theotokos with him: Rejoice, thou who art full of grace, the Lord is with thee.[45]

The special features of the services on the feast of the Annunciation are determined by the day on which it falls. If on a Sunday or Monday in Lent, the All-night Vigil preceding it begins with Vespers; if on any other day of the week—with Compline, because Vespers then combines with the Hours. At Matins on the day of this feast, the Polyeleos is sung, excepting when the Annunciation falls on the first day of Easter. In that case, the Polyeleos is omitted, the canon of the feast is sung together with the Paschal canon, and the Gospel of the Annunciation is read after the sixth ode of the canon. The combination of the two feasts is called *Kyriopascha*, i.e., "the Lord's Pascha." The Hours are the same for the Annunciation as for the day on which the feast falls: on Saturdays and Sundays, the ordinary Hours; on other days, the Lenten Hours; on Holy Friday, the Royal Hours; and through the Paschal Week, the Paschal Hours. On the days on which the Lenten or the Royal Hours are prescribed, the Liturgy is celebrated after Vespers in combination with this service. If the Annunciation falls on any Sunday of Lent except Palm Sunday, or on Thursday or Saturday of the Holy Week, the Liturgy of Basil the Great is given; on all other days that of John Chrysostom.

The Day of the Holy and Most Glorious Apostles Peter and Paul

The feast of the Apostles Peter and Paul is celebrated on the 29th of June. On the following day the faithful congregate to celebrate the Twelve Apostles. The special feature of this feast is the fast which precedes it, beginning one week after Pentecost and ending on the vigil of St. Peter's day. This fast the Church designates as "the Apostles'," but the people call it simply "Peter s Fast." It is observed in memory of the fact that the Apostles fasted before they went forth to preach the Gospel.

The Transfiguration of Our Lord and Saviour Jesus Christ

The Transfiguration of our Lord is celebrated on the 6th of August. It is the rule to bring to the churches on this day, for consecration, the first-fruits of fruit-bearing trees. In the East they bring grapes; in Russia they bring apples.[46]

The substance of this feast's hymns is expressed in the troparion for the day: "Thou wast transfigured on the mountain, O Christ our God, showing to Thy disciples Thy glory as each one could endure; shine forth Thou on us, who are sinners all, Thy light ever-unending. Through the prayers of the Theotokos. O Light-giver, glory to Thee."

The Dormition of the Mother of God

For the worthy celebration of the feast of the Dormition we prepare by a fast beginning on the 1st of August and lasting until the day of the feast — the 15th of August. The Church calls it "Dormition Fast," but the people also give it the name of "Lady s Fast," because it is observed in honor of Our Lady, the Queen of Heaven.

The substance of the Dormition hymns is expressed in the troparion for the day: "In giving birth thou didst retain thy virginity; in thy dormition thou didst not forsake the world, O Theotokos. Thou wast translated unto life, since thou art the Mother of Life, and by thine intercessions dost thou deliver our souls from death."

The Beheading of the Honorable Glorious Prophet and Forerunner, John the Baptist

This event is commemorated on the 29th of August. As men, on this day, once forgot righteousness and conscience in the midst of feasting, it is ordered that this day should be a day of fasting, as a reminder to us to look well after the purity of our souls in the midst of pleasures and amusements.

The Procession of the Holy and Life Giving Cross

On this day, the 1st of August, two feasts are combined: (1) the bringing forth of the holy and life-giving Cross, and (2) the celebration of the All-merciful Saviour, Christ God and the Holy Virgin Mary, His Mother. This is one of the lesser feasts. In Constantinople, on the 1st of August, the Life-giving Cross used to be brought forth from the palace and carried to the church of St. Sophia, and the ceremony of consecrating the waters was performed on this occasion. After this, for fifteen days, the Cross was carried through the streets of the city, with prayers for the preservation of the people from mortal epidemics and pestilence, because at this time of the year there usually was much sickness among the people; then the Cross was carried back into the palace. In 1164, the second celebration was added, in memory of two victories gained on this day: one by the Greek Emperor Manuel over the Saracens, and one by the Russian Prince Andreas Bogoliubsky over the Bulgars.

The special feature of the feast is the bringing forth of the Cross for veneration. This is done as on the day of the Exaltation. Only the ceremony of elevation itself is nowhere performed. After the Liturgy and sometimes after Matins, processions go to lakes, ponds and rivers where the lesser blessing of the waters takes place. The lesser blessing differs from the great blessing on the day of the Epiphany, in that the prayer recited by the priest is shorter,[47] and at the immersion of the Cross the verse, "Save O Lord, Thy people," is sung, and not, "When Thou wast baptized in the Jordan, O Lord."

Movable Feasts and Fasts

All the movable days of worship are connected with the greatest Christian feast, Easter, "the Day of the Pascha." Some of them are a preparation for the worthy celebration of this feast; others continue the festivities, making us sensible of its fruits.

The preparation for the feast consists of two fasts, that of Great Lent, beginning on the Monday of the first week and ending with the Friday of the sixth, and the fast of the Holy Week. These two fasts are united by two days of which one, Saturday, is sacred to the memory of the Resurrection of Lazarus, and the other, Sunday, to that of Christ's entry into Jerusalem. Both fasts together are called "the Great Fast," or "Lent." Over and above these weeks, three weeks are set apart as a preparation for Lent. Thus the whole time of preparation for the Paschal Feast comprises ten weeks.

The Paschal Feast lasts seven days. But the festivities do not end with these. The hymns in honor of the Resurrection are sung up to the day of the Ascension. Then for two more Sundays, the Church speaks of the fruits which the Resurrection bore for our good: one is sacred to the memory of the Descent of the Holy Spirit upon the Apostles, and the other commemorates all the Saints who have obtained the Kingdom of Heaven through faith in the Lord crucified and risen from the dead.

THE WEEKS OF PREPARATION FOR LENT

Lent is a time of penance, and as penance requires a sense of one's unworthiness, hope in the mercy of the Lord, fear of judgment, and a readiness to forgive others, all these feelings must be aroused in us before the beginning of Lent.

Three weeks before Lent, on Sunday, the parable of the Publican and the Pharisee is read, and in the Matins hymns the meaning of it is explained, which is a lesson of humility. This Sunday is called, "the Sunday of the

Publican and Pharisee," and from it until the Sunday of the fifth week of Lent, after the hymn, "Having beheld the Resurrection of Christ..." penitential troparia are sung, inculcating humility. Besides this, that we may be taught still more clearly not to take pride in and boast of fulfilling the law, as the Pharisee of the parable boasted of keeping the fasts, the fast of the Wednesday and Friday is remitted for the following week.

Penitential Troparia

The doors of repentance do Thou open to me, O Giver of life, for my spirit waketh at dawn toward Thy holy temple, bearing a temple of the body all defiled. But in Thy compassion, cleanse it by the loving-kindness of Thy mercy.

Guide me in the paths of salvation, O Theotokos, for I have defiled my soul with shameful sins, and have wasted all my life in slothfulness, but by thine intercessions deliver me from all uncleanness.

When I think of the multitude of evil things I have done, I, a wretched one, I tremble at the fearful day of judgment; but trusting in the mercy of Thy loving-kindness, like David do I cry unto Thee: Have mercy on me, O God, according to Thy great mercy.[48]

On the following Sunday, during the Liturgy, the parable of the Prodigal Son is read, which teaches us, having repented of our sins, not to despair of our salvation, but to trust in the mercy of the Lord, our Heavenly Father. This Sunday is called the Sunday of the Prodigal Son. The essence of the hymns of the day is expressed in the Psalm: "By the rivers of Babylon, there we sat down and we wept when we remembered Sion." This Psalm is sung at Matins after the Polyeleos Psalms.

On the Sunday following that of the Prodigal Son, the lesson from the Gospel is that on the Day of Judgment, that we, in trusting to God's mercy, may not forget His justice and may not lapse into carelessness. This Sunday is called, "the Sunday of Meat Fare," because with it ends the eating of meat. On the day before—Saturday—the Church commemorates, i.e., prays for, all our deceased forefathers, fathers and brethren, for whom the time of repentance is past, and who can obtain the mercy of God only through the prayers of the living. The Matins service on this Saturday consists mostly of prayers for the rest of their souls.

This Sunday is followed by the "Cheesefare Week," which is the vestibule to Lent. It has received this name, because, all through it the use of butter, cheese, and eggs is allowed. In all the hymns of this week the Fall of Adam is referred to and it is shown that it was caused by intemperance. On Wednesday and Friday of this week there is no Liturgy, but only a Lenten service. The last day of the week, Sunday, is called, "the Sunday of Cheese-Fare," because with it ends the eating of butter, cheese and eggs. The Gospel lesson, at the Liturgy of the day, commands us to forgive one another's sins. This is why Christians on this day ask one another's forgiveness for mutual offenses, and make efforts to become mutually reconciled. Hence, the day is called "Forgiveness Sunday."

PECULIARITIES OF LENTEN SERVICES

The general feature of Lenten services is their increased duration with lessened splendor: in particular, a limited number of joyful and triumphal hymns, subdued light, less frequent drawing away of the curtain and opening of the royal gates. Most of the services are performed with the royal gates closed and consist of the reading of Psalms and penitential prayers, with frequent prostrations. At every service the penitential prayer of Ephraim the Syrian is recited with prostrations: "O Lord and Master of my life, a spirit of idleness, despondency, ambition, and idle talking give me not. But rather a spirit of chastity, humble-mindedness, patience, and love bestow upon me Thy servant. Yea, O Lord King, grant me to see my failings and not condemn my brother. For blessed art Thou unto the ages of ages. Amen." At Matins, every day except Saturday and Sunday, "Alleluia" is sung instead of "God is the Lord and hath appeared unto us."

The Liturgy being a joyful, triumphal service, it is celebrated during Lent only on Saturdays and Sundays; on the other days only the Typica service is performed. Yet, in order that Christians may not be deprived for long of the privilege of partaking of the Sacrament of the Eucharist, it is permitted to give communion on certain days at Vespers, using *Presanctified Gifts.* Such a Vespers service at which the faithful may receive communion is called, "the Liturgy of the Presanctified," also the Liturgy of Gregory the Great, because the ritual of it was written down by the Roman Pope, Saint Gregory the Great.

There is a special combination of services prescribed for Lent. The evening service consists of Compline; the morning service of Matins and the First Hour; the noon service, of the Third, Sixth and Ninth Hours, the Typica, and Vespers, combined on certain days with the Liturgy of the Presanctified.

THE LENTEN HOURS

The peculiarity of the offices of the Hours in Lent consists in this, that at every Hour: (1) after the three psalms the kathisma is read; (2) in the place of the troparia for the day, special troparia are read, indicating the events commemorated in the service for the given Hour; (3) before the concluding prayer of the Hour, the penitential prayer of St. Ephraim is recited, with prostrations. At the Sixth Hour, over and above all the above mentioned, a paremia is read.

Troparion of the First Hour

In the morning, hearken unto my voice, O my King and my God.

Of the Third Hour

O Lord, Who didst send down Thy Most-holy Spirit at the third hour upon Thine apostles: take Him not from us, O Good One, but renew Him in us who pray unto Thee.

Of the Sixth Hour

O Thou Who on the sixth day and in the sixth hour didst nail to the Cross Adam's daring sin in Paradise, tear asunder also the handwriting of our sins, O Christ God, and save us.

Of the Ninth Hour

O Thou Who at the ninth hour for our sake didst taste of death in the flesh, mortify our carnal mind, O Christ God, and save us.[49]

THE LITURGY OF THE PRESANCTIFIED

The Liturgy of the Presanctified is celebrated on those days of Lent when the contrition proper to the season does not allow for the triumphal gladness conveyed by the full Liturgy, yet the memories of the day demand the comfort of the Communion Sacrament. Such days are the Wednesdays and Fridays in Lent, the first three days of Holy Week, and all the days on which falls the feast of some Saint, in whose honor the Polyeleos is prescribed. At this Liturgy the gifts are not consecrated, but the faithful who receive communion partake of the Gifts which have been consecrated at the preceding Liturgy of Basil the Great or of John Chrysostom, and havr been preserved in an ark on the altar. Therefore, the Liturgy of the Presanctified consists only in the bringing out of the Holy Gifts, the preparation for communion, the act of communion, and the thanksgiving for communion. This service is combined with that of Vespers. However, as catechumens may be present at Vespers, but only the faithful may witness the Liturgy, therefore, at the end of the Vespers service, before the Holy Gifts are transferred to the altar, the catechumens are bidden to depart.

Until the Vespers entry, the service proceeds as usual, with the only difference that it begins with the benediction of the Kingdom of the Holy Trinity, as when the complete Liturgy is celebrated: "Blessed is the Kingdom of the Father, and of the Son, and of the Holy Spirit." The initiatory exclamation of the priest is followed by the introductory

Psalm, the Great Ectenia, the kathisma, divided into three sections or Antiphons by the Small Ectenia, recited twice, the Psalm, "Lord, I have cried," with sticheræ, and the hymn, "O Gentle Light." Before this latter hymn is sung, the royal gates are opened and the priest enters with the censer, or—if it be a day on which a reading from the Gospels is appointed—with the Gospel. After the entry the prokimenon is sung, the royal gates are closed, and two paremiæ for the day are read; on feast-days the paremia of the feast is added. After the first paremia the royal gates are again opened and the prokimenon of the first paremia is sung. Then the priest takes in his hands a censer and a lighted candle and exclaims: "Wisdom! Aright!," to arouse the attention of the worshippers, and makes the sign of the Cross over them with the censer and the candle, with the words: "the Light of Christ shineth upon all," in token that the Old Testament Saints, whose words are read in the paremiae, were also illumined by the same light as the New Testament man, that they lived and were saved by faith in the coming Christ as we are saved by faith in Christ. At this moment the faithful worship Christ, the Light of Truth, with a prostration. This ceremony is a survival of the ancient custom of making the sign of the Cross with a candle during Lent over the catechumens who were preparing for baptism before Easter; it was done in anticipation of the illumination which the catechumens were to receive through this Sacrament. After the ceremony, the royal gates are closed once more, and the second paremia is read.

After the paremia, in order to arouse more strongly the feeling of penitence, the worshippers listen prostrate to the Verses of the Psalm which were sung before the introit, and which now are sung again with deep contrition: "Let my prayer be set forth as incense before Thee; the lifting up of my hands as an evening sacrifice." — "Lord, I have cried unto Thee, hearken unto me; attend unto the voice of my supplication, when I cry unto Thee."— "Set O Lord, a watch before my mouth, and a door of enclosure round about my lips."—"Incline not my heart to words of evil, to make excuse with excuses in sins." Then the worshippers express their repentance by repeating the prayer of Ephraim the Syrian, with three prostrations. Here follow readings from the Gospel and the Apostle, if such are prescribed; if they are not, the Triple Ectenia is recited. The general prayers of the Vespers service end with the Ectenia for the Catechumens and with the latter departing from the church. The faithful remain, and the special prayers of the Liturgy begin.

The Liturgy begins with two Small Ecteniæ, each ending with the exclamation, "Wisdom!" after which the Cherubic Hymn is sung during the transfer of the Holy Gifts: "Now the hosts of Heaven minister with us invisibly; for behold the King of Glory entereth. Behold, the finished Mystical Sacrifice is being escorted in [literally, *upborne on lances*]. With faith and love let us draw nigh, that we may become partakers of Life everlasting. Alleluia, alleluia, alleluia." At the words, "borne on high" the singing is suspended; the priest enters through the northern door, bearing on his head the paten, on which repose the Pre-sanctified Gifts, and in his hand the chalice with the wine, and enters the sanctuary through the royal gates, without speaking. With a prostration The faithful worship Christ, Who passed before them in the Sacrament. After the priest has entered the sanctuary, the royal gates are closed, the curtain is drawn shut, and the choir takes up and ends the Cherubic Hymn.

After the transfer of the Holy Gifts, the faithful prepare for communion. The Triple Ectenia is recited, the Lord's Prayer is chanted, the priest offers "Peace be unto all," and proclaims "The Presanctified Holy Things are for the holy," to which the faithful respond by singing, "One is holy, One is Lord, Jesus Christ, to the glory of God the Father, Amen." Then the Communion Hymn is sung: "O taste and see that the Lord is good. Alleluia, alleluia, alleluia."

The communion of the celebrants and the laymen, the giving of thanks, and the dismissal take place as usual. However, instead of "Blessed is He that cometh in the name of the Lord," the choir sings the hymn: "I will bless the Lord at all times; His praise shall continually be in my mouth. The heavenly Bread, and the Cup of Life; O taste and see that the Lord is good. Alleluia, alleluia, alleluia." And, when the priest descends from the ambo, he reads a prayer in which he asks that the Lord may "Grant us also. . . to fight the good fight, to finish the course of the Fast, to preserve inviolate the Faith, to crush under foot the heads of invisible serpents, to be accounted victors over sin,å and uncondemned to attain unto and worship the holy Resurrection."

SPECIAL FEATURES OF THE SERVICES
IN EACH WEEK OF GREAT LENT

Each of the successive weeks of Great Lent presents some special feature in the services. At Great Compline, the first four days of the first week, the penitential canon composed by St. Andrew of Crete is read. The troparia of this canon call our attention to the virtues and transgressions of the men who are spoken of in Holy Scripture, and urge us to imitate the former and shun the example of the latter. The burden of the canon is the prayer, "Have mercy on me, O God, have mercy on me." On the Wednesday and Thursday, to this canon is added that to St. Mary of Egypt, who was at first a great sinner, then a great penitent and ascetic. This latter canon was also composed by St. Andrew of Crete, and teaches us not to despair of our salvation, but to labor at our self-improvement, while trusting in the help of God. This Compline office is also called *Ephymnion*—a Greek word which means, "the burden or refrain of a song."

On the Saturday of the first week there is a celebration in honor of St. Theodore Tyro, Martyr. It begins already on Friday at Vespers, when, after the Liturgy of the Pre-sanctified, a prayer is said for the blessing of the wheat food (*Kólivo, Kutyá*—boiled wheat with honey.) This celebration commemorates the following occasion:

The Greek Emperor Julian, apostate from the Faith, wishing to pollute the Christians by the use of food forbidden by the Church, secretly ordered that every article of food placed for sale on the markets in the first week of Lent should be sprinkled with the blood of animals sacrificed to the idols. But St. Theodore appeared to the bishop of the city in a vision, made known to him Julian's secret order, and advised that the Christians should buy no eatables in the markets during the whole week, but live on boiled wheat with honey.

On the first Sunday of Great Lent, the "Triumph of Orthodoxy" is celebrated, in memory of the restoration of the veneration of holy icons under the Empress Theodora (862 AD). The special feature of the day's service consists in this, that, in Cathedral churches, before the Liturgy and after the Hours, or just before the end of the Liturgy, the celebrants come into the middle of the church, bearing icons of the Saviour and of the Mother of God, and, having placed them on lecterns, perform before them a special service with singing, consisting chiefly of petitions that the Lord may establish Christians in the true belief and incline apostates and heretics to return to the right path. At the end of the service, the deacon, in a loud voice, recites the Creed, to impress on Orthodox Christians the doctrine which they are to hold. After which he enumerates all the false doctrines, pronounces anathema (i.e., separation from the Church or exclusion from the community of Orthodox Christians) against all those who receive them, and "eternal memory" for the defenders of the faith. The service concludes with the proclamation of "length of days" to Orthodox Patriarchs, to the clergy, and to all Orthodox Christians, and with the petition that the Lord may keep them firm in the true faith, and convert and bring to the knowledge of eternal truth the traducers and blasphemers of the Orthodox Faith and Church and those who rebel against them. Then the hymn, "We praise Thee, O God," is sung, during which the worshippers express their reverence for icons by veneration and kisses.

On the third Sunday of Lent, at Matins, after the Great Doxology, the Cross is brought out into the middle of the church as on the day of the Exaltation, for veneration, to the singing of the hymn, "Before Thy Cross we bow down, O Master, and Thy holy Resurrection we glorify." The Cross remains in the church all through the week, but the veneration takes place only on Monday and Wednesday, at the office of the First Hour, and on Friday after the service of the Hours, when the Cross is taken back into the sanctuary. The week following this ceremony on the third Sunday bears the name of the "Week of the Veneration of the Cross."

On Thursday of the fifth week (following the fourth Sunday), at Matins, the entire penitential canon of St Andrew of Crete is read together with the canon in honor of St. Mary of Egypt. On this day the Liturgy of the Presanctified is celebrated.

On Saturday of the fifth week, at Matins, an Akathist in honor of the Virgin is read, in remembrance of the deliverance on this day of Constantinople from the invading Persians and Avars in the seventh century through the intercession of the Virgin, whose icon was carried around the walls of the city.

SPECIAL FEATURES OF THE SERVICES
ON LAZARUS SATURDAY AND PALM SUNDAY

These two days are the preliminary to the fast of Holy Week. The Saturday commemorates the raising of Lazarus from the dead, and is called "the Resurrection of Lazarus."

Because this event manifested the divine might of Christ, and prepared His solemn entrance into Jerusalem, and, on the other hand, gave the assurance that all the dead should rise, therefore, at Matins are sung the Sunday troparia, "The assembly of angels was amazed," and the hymn,

"Having beheld the Resurrection of Christ," while the prayers for the souls of the dead, usually sung on Saturdays, are omitted.

The Sunday following on this Saturday commemorates the solemn entry of Christ into Jerusalem, and is one of the Twelve Feasts.

At Matins, after the reading from the Gospels, the consecration of the palms takes place (in our country budding willow branches are substituted for the palm branches). All through the singing of the canon, the worshippers hold in their hands these branches and lighted candles. From this ceremony the day has the name of Palm Sunday. The essence of the hymns of this day and the meaning of the ceremony of consecrating the palms are expressed in the troparion of the feast: "In confirming the common Resurrection, O Christ God, Thou didst raise up Lazarus from the dead before Thy Passion. Wherefore, we also, like the children bearing the symbols of victory, cry to Thee, the Vanquisher of death: Hosanna in the highest; blessed is He that cometh in the name of the Lord."

SPECIAL FEATURES OF THE SERVICES
ON THE FIRST THREE DAYS OF PASSION WEEK

The Monday, Tuesday and Wednesday of Passion (Holy) Week commemorate the last communings of Jesus with the people and His disciples. These communings make up the substance of nearly all the hymns of these days.[50] At Matins after the Alleluia, instead of "God is the Lord," is sung the troparion: "Behold, the Bridegroom cometh at midnight, and blessed is that servant whom He shall find watching; but unworthy is he whom He shall find heedless. Beware, therefore, O my soul, lest thou be weighed down with sleep; lest thou be given up to death, and be shut out from the kingdom. But rouse thyself and cry: Holy, Holy, Holy art Thou, O God; through the Theotokos, have mercy on us." After the canon is sung the hymn: "Thy bridal chamber do I see, O my Saviour, adorned, and no wedding garment have I that I may enter there. Illumine the robe of my soul, O Light-giver, and save me." On these three days the Liturgy of the Presanctified is celebrated, with readings from the Gospel. The Gospel is read also at Matins. And besides all this, in order to bring before us more vividly and fully the entire life of Christ, the Church prescribes to read all the four Gospels through on these days, at the Offices of the Hours. From the importance of the events commemorated, all the days of the Passion Week are called "holy" and "great."

SPECIAL FEATURES OF THE SERVICE ON GREAT AND HOLY THURSDAY

The service of Holy Thursday commemorates the washing of the disciples' feet, the Mystical Supper, Christ's praying in the garden of Gethsemane, and His betrayal by Judas. The special features of the day are the following: A paremia is read at the First Hour; the Liturgy of Basil the Great is celebrated in combination with Vespers; at the Liturgy, instead of the Cherubic Hymn, the Communion Prayer, the verse during the act of communion, and the hymn, "Let our mouth be filled with praise," the choir sings: "Receive me this day, O Son of God, as a partaker of Thy Mystical Supper."

In Cathedral churches, after the prayer which the priest descends from the ambo to recite, the ceremony of the washing of the feet is performed. The bishop comes forth and steps on an ambo placed in the middle of the church (the robing platform); there he takes his seat in an armchair before a lectern on which lies a Gospel. Then the deacon leads forth from the Sanctuary twelve priests, two by two, and they take seats on both sides of the bishop in two rows, from the platform to the royal gates. During this time the choir sings stichera in which the washing of the disciples' feet by the Lord at the Last Supper is referred to. When all the twelve priests, representing the disciples at the Supper, are in their places, the deacon recites the Great Ectenia, adding a petition that, "it (i.e., the washing) will be for the washing away of the defilement of our sins, let us pray to the Lord." During the recital of the ectenia, the bishop and the priests remain seated; when it is concluded the bishop alone rises, offers up a prayer, that "the Lord may deign to let the contact of this water wash us of all spiritual impurity and to preserve us from the spiritual serpent, which striveth to bite our heel," and sits down again. Then, all the celebrants remaining seated, begins the reading of the Gospel, telling how Christ, at the Mystical Supper, washed His disciples' feet. As the deacon utters the words, "He riseth from supper," the bishop rises; at the words, "and laid aside His garments," he lays aside his episcopal vestments: the panagia, the pectoral Cross, the omophorion, the thigh-shield and the saccos. During the disrobing the deacon keeps repeating the words, "and laid aside His garments." The deacon reads on: "and took a towel and girded Himself," the bishop then girds himself with a towel. The deacon reads, "After that He poureth water into a basin," and the bishop pours water from an ewer into a basin. When the deacon reads "and began to wash the disciples' feet, and to wipe them with the towel wherewith He was girded," the bishop washes the feet of the twelve priests, beginning with him who sits first on the left hand side and ending with him who sits first on the right hand side. The order of the washing is as follows: the bishop pours water thrice from his hand on each priest's foot, wipes it with the towel and kisses the priest's hand; and he whose foot has been washed, kisses the bishop's miter and hand. While the feet of eleven of the priests are washed, the deacon keeps repeating the words, "and began to wash the disciples' feet and to wipe them with the towel wherewith He was girded." As the deacon reads, "Then cometh He to Simon Peter and Peter said unto him," the bishop approaches the priest who sits first on the right hand side; the priest rises from his seat and says in the words of the Gospel: "Lord, dost Thou wash my feet?" The bishop replies, also in the words of the Gospel: "What I do, thou knowest not now, but thou shalt know hereafter." The priest continues to speak in the words of the Gospel: "Thou shalt never wash my feet." The bishop replies: "If I wash thee not, thou hast no part with me." Then the priest says: "Lord, not my feet only, but my hands and my head," pointing to his hands and head, and resumes his seat. The bishop replies in the words of the Gospel: "He that is washed needeth not but to wash his feet, but is clean every whit: and ye are clean, but not all," and washes the priests foot, after which he returns to his place on the platform and takes off the towel, and the deacon reads the end of the Gospel: "For He knew who should betray Him; therefore said He, 'Ye are not all clean.'" The choir now sings "Glory to Thee, our God, glory to Thee." Then the deacon again invites those present to listen attentively to the Gospel, and continues reading: "After He had washed their feet, and had taken His garments." The words, "and had taken His garments," are repeated many times, while the bishop resumes his vestments. As the deacon reads the words, "and was set down again," the bishop sits down and all the priests rise to their feet. Then the bishop himself reads the end of the Gospel: "I have given you an example, that ye should do as I have done to you." The bishop then rises and offers a prayer, that "the Lord, may wash away all impurity from our souls, and that we, having washed away the dust of transgressions that did cling to our souls, may "wipe one another with the towel of love and gain the strength to please God." Then the bishop enters the sanctuary and goes on with the Liturgy.

At the Church of the Dormition in Moscow and in the Lavra of the Caves at Kiev (*Kievo-Pecherskaya Lavra*) there takes place on Holy Thursday the consecration of the myrrh or chrism which is used in all the churches in Russia for the Sacraments of Confirmation, at the consecration of churches and Antiminses, and at the coronation of a Tsar. The preparation of the ingredients begins from the week of the Veneration of the Cross. The ingredients are: olive oil, wine, sweet-smelling oils, and various kinds of incense and herbs (thirty in all). The oil is emblematic of mercy, the wine of Christ's Blood, and the perfumes symbolize the manifold gifts of the Holy Spirit. From Monday of the Holy Week, the mixture of oil and wine simmers in kettles to the continuous reading of the Gospels. On Wednesday the aromatic ingredients are added and the myrrh is poured out of the kettles into vessels. On Thursday before the Liturgy, the bishop and priests, in full canonicals, transfer the vessels containing the new myrrh and a vessel containing last year's myrrh to the church, and place them on and around the Table of Oblations. At the great procession with the Holy Gifts, the vessels with the myrrh are also transferred from the Table of Oblations to the altar. The vessel with last year's myrrh is placed upon the altar; the vessels with the new myrrh are placed around it. After the exclamation "And may the mercies of the Lord, our God and Saviour, Jesus Christ, be with you all!," the consecration of the myrrh takes place. The bishop blesses each vessel thrice with the words, "In the name of the Father and of the Son and of the Holy Spirit," then prays that the Lord "may send down upon the myrrh the grace of the Holy Spirit, and make it a spiritual anointment, a repository of life, a sanctification of bodies and souls, an oil of gladness." After the Ectenia of Supplication and commemoration of all the Saints, the myrrh is taken into the repository of sacred vessels. There, into each vessel of new myrrh are poured a few drops of the old myrrh, and the vessel which holds the latter is replenished with new myrrh. This is done in token of the uninterrupted connection of the Russian Church with the Greek, from which she received the grace of priesthood in the person of her first bishop and also received the first consecrated myrrh.

Special Features of the Services
On Great and Holy Friday

The services on Holy Friday commemorate the Passion of Christ. Matins begins at the second hour of night (eight p.m. on Thursday, as we count time). There is no kathisma, but after the Great Ectenia and the "Alleluia," the twelve Gospels are read which narrate the Passion of Christ, beginning with His last discourse with His disciples at the Last Supper, and ending with His entombing in the garden of Joseph of Arimathæa. Between the readings, hymns are sung in which Judas' treason and the Jews' malice are denounced, then the Triodion and sticheræ are chanted. The service ends with the ectenia.

During the reading of the Gospels, the faithful stand with lighted candles in their hands. This service is called "the succession of the holy and saving passions of Our Lord Jesus Christ"—familiarly "the Passions." There is no Liturgy on Holy Friday. The Royal Hours are read, in which the Psalms, the troparia, the paremiæ, the Epistles, and Gospels all have reference to Christ's Passion. Vespers begins at the tenth hour of the day (three p.m.). At this service, after the introit, are read three paremiæ and lessons from an Epistle and a Gospel. (The Gospel reading is comprised of the narratives of the three Evangelists—Matthew, Luke and John of the Passion of Christ, from the conference of the Jews to the Saviour's death.) After the sticheræ the *Epitaphion* (*Plaschanítsa*) is brought out of the sanctuary and placed in the middle of the church. This is a painting, generally on canvas (or an embroidery or tapestry), representing Christ entombed, in memory of the taking down from the Cross of the body of Christ. This ceremony takes place to the singing of the troparion, "The noble Joseph, having taken Thy most pure Body down from the Tree and wrapped It in pure linen and covered It with spices, laid It in a new tomb." The canvas is laid out on a table, and all present adore it and kiss the wounds of Christ in the side, the hands, and the feet. If the feast of the Annunciation happens on this day, Vespers take place earlier, combined with the Liturgy of John Chrysostom, and the Epitaphion is brought out at Small Compline.

Special Features of the Services on Great and Holy Saturday

On Holy Saturday, after "God is the Lord" and the troparia, the 118th Psalm (the 17th *kathisma*) is Sung: "Blessed are the blameless in the way, who walk in the law of the Lord," verse by verse. The verses of the Psalm are divided by refrains which are called *praises* because they contain a glorification of the dead and entombed Lord. All present during this time hold lighted candles in their hands. The Psalm is followed by the Sunday troparia and canon. During the canon the celebrants don the full, sacerdotal vestments, and after the Great Doxology take up the Epitaphion to the singing of the funeral Trisagion, and carry it in procession either outside around the church, or inside around the Sanctuary and church, in memory of the entombing of the Lord. When it is restored to its place in the middle of the church, the ecteniæ are recited, the paremias are read, as well as the Epistle and Gospel, then follows the veneration before the Epitaphion.

The Liturgy is celebrated on this day after the rite of Basil the Great, and is combined with Vespers. As the latter service has reference to the next day (Sunday), the hymns commemorating the entombing of Christ alternate during the Liturgy with those belonging to the Sunday service. After the evening entry, which on this day takes place with the Gospel, fifteen paremiaæ are read containing prophecies and prototypes of salvation through the passion and resurrection of Christ. The lesson from the Apostle (the Epistle reading) tells us that through Baptism we are entombed together with Christ. Before the Gospel lesson, the choir, instead of "Alleluia," sings the prokimenon "Arise, O God, judge the earth, for Thou shalt have an inheritance among all the nations." While this prokimenon is sung, the celebrants change their vestments (from a dark color to a festal color) and the decorations of the church are changed likewise. The Gospel reading tells of Christ rising from the dead. Instead of "It is meet," the eirmos of the 9th ode of the Matins canon is sung, and instead of the Cherubic Hymn, the hymn: "Let all mortal flesh keep silence, and stand with fear and trembling; and let it take no thought for any earthly thing. For the King of kings and Lord of lords draweth nigh to be sacrificed and given as food to the faithful. Before Him go the choirs of angels with all the principalities and powers, the many-eyed cherubim and the six-winged seraphim, covering their faces and crying aloud the hymn: Alleluia, alleluia, alleluia."

The Liturgy ends with the blessing of bread, wine and oil, for the restoration of the worshippers' strength; for, according to ancient custom, they should spend this entire day and the night following in the church. After the service ends, the reading of the Book of the Acts of the Apostles begins and continues until the next service begins.

During the hour before midnight, all lampadas and candelabra are lit, and, to the toll of the bells, the midnight service begins, during which the canon for Holy Saturday is sung. When this service is concluded, the celebrants silently transport the Epitaphion from the middle of the church through the royal gates into the sanctuary, and there lay it upon the altar, where it remains until the end of the Paschal festival, in memory of Christ's forty days' sojourn on earth after His resurrection from the dead. Then all reverently await the stroke of midnight.

SPECIAL FEATURES OF THE SERVICES
ON THE DAY OF HOLY PASCHA

At the stroke of twelve, in the night from Saturday to Sunday, begins the celebration in honor of the Resurrection of Christ. This feast is called the Pascha—by the name of the Old Testament feast instituted in commemoration of the Jews' deliverance out of Egyptian bondage— because that feast was the prototype of the Christian feast. Then the blood of the lamb with which the doors of Hebrew dwellings were smeared preserved the Jews from the angel who was smiting the Egyptian first-born with death. Now Christ, in dying on the Cross for our sins, like unto an immaculate Lamb, delivered us by His resurrection from the bondage of sin and the devil. As we know of no event more joyful and radiant, the Church names this day "the Feast of Feasts" and "the triumph of triumphs." The substance of all the hymns of this feast is expressed in the troparion "Christ is risen from the dead, trampling down death by death, and upon those in the tombs bestowing life."

At midnight the celebrants, carrying the Cross, the Gospel and icons, escorted and followed by all the faithful, to the ringing of the bells and the swinging of censers, go forth in procession and walk around the church on the outside, singing: "Thy Resurrection, O Christ Saviour, the angels hymn in the heavens; vouchsafe also us on earth with pure hearts to glorify Thee." The procession reminds us how the myrrh-bearing women went to the Sepulcher in the dim morning, intending to anoint the body of Christ with myrrh. It stops at the vestibule or on the porch before the western doors which at this moment are closed. Here the priest blesses the beginning of Matins: "Glory to the holy, consubstantial, life giving, and indivisible Trinity." In response to this, the troparion, "Christ is risen," is sung many times. While the troparion is being sung, the western doors are opened and the procession enters the church. The Matins service begins in the vestibule, in memory of the women having received the first news of the resurrection at the entrance of the Sepulcher. The entire Matins service consists of ecteniæ and Paschal hymns. First, the Great Ectenia is recited; after that, the entire canon is sung, then the eirmoi and the troparia. Each ode of the canon ends with the Small Ectenia and after each ode, every part of the church is censed. After the canon, the choir sings, "Let every breath praise the Lord," with verses, and the hymn, "Let God arise," with sticheræ. When the choir sings the stichera, "Let us embrace one another, let us say brethren even to them that hate us, let us forgive all things for the sake of the Resurrection," all Christians exchange brotherly kisses, with the mutual greeting, "Christ is risen!"—"Truly He is risen!" After which follow the Triple Ectenia, the Ectenia of Supplication, and dismissal.

The Hours offices consist exclusively of Paschal hymns.

The Liturgy follows immediately after Matins. The Gospel lesson read is one that tells not of the Resurrection of Christ, but of His pre-eternal birth from God the Father and of His Divinity, because Christ, by His Resurrection, manifested His Divinity. It is customary on this day to read the Gospel in several languages, so that all may hear the glad tidings, each in his own tongue.

Vespers also consists mainly of Paschal hymns. The entry is made with the Gospel, and the Gospel reading tells of the Resurrection.

The entire week is one feast. Therefore, the services are alike on all days, differing only in that, from Monday to Saturday, the procession takes place not in the beginning, but at the end of the Matins service, and no Gospel is read at Vespers. During the Paschal week, all the doors of the sanctuary remain open and the curtain drawn aside, in token that Christ, by His resurrection, hath opened to us the doors of the Kingdom of Heaven.

One of the special features of the feast of the Pascha is the consecration of bread stamped with the image of the Cross, or, sometimes, of the Resurrection, and named by the Greek name *Ártos*. The Artos is consecrated at the close of the Paschal Liturgy in memory of Christ risen, Who is "the Bread of Life Eternal descended from Heaven and nourishing us with the food of His divine mercies." On Saturday, after the Liturgy, it is broken and distributed in the place of Antidoron among the faithful who partake of it, taking home pieces for those who were not present in church.[51] This rite refers to the Apostles' custom of laying bread aside at their meals in memory of Christ, when He had ascended to Heaven. On the first Pascha day, the Church consecrates eggs, cheese and meat, thus proclaiming the end of Lent. In our country it is customary to bring to the churches home-made *Kulítch* (large round loaves of rich, cake-like bread) to be sprinkled with holy water, and for friends to exchange the gift of a red-dyed egg. The egg symbolizes the renovated life, received through the Blood of Christ the Saviour.

SPECIAL FEATURES OF THE SERVICES FROM THE PASCHAL WEEK TO ALL-SAINTS' SUNDAY

The Paschal hymns are sung through all the forty days until the feast of the Ascension. The first Sunday after Pascha is called the Sunday of the Apostle Thomas, also the Anti-Paschal and the Renewal Sunday. The first name is given to this day because it is dedicated to the memory of the Lord's appearing to the disciples, among whom was Thomas; the second and third names refer to the fact that on that day, for the first time after Pascha Sunday, the celebration of the Resurrection is repeated and renewed. On the Tuesday of this week, and, in some localities on the Monday also, a commemoration of the dead takes place, which is called a "joyful" one *(Rádonitsa)*, because the prayers for the rest of the souls of the departed begin with the joyful tidings of the Resurrection. On the second Sunday, the service is in honor of the Myrrh-bearing Women, Joseph of Arimathæa, and Nicodemus. The third Sunday commemorates the healing of the paralytic; the fourth, the conversation with the Samaritan woman; the fifth, the healing of the man blind from birth. On Wednesday of the sixth week, the Paschal festival is declared ended with closing prayers, and the singing of the Paschal hymns ceases.

On Thursday of the sixth week, which is the fortieth day from Pascha Sunday, is commemorated the Ascension of Christ into Heaven. The substance of the hymns for this day is expressed in the troparion: "Thou hast ascended in glory, O Christ our God, having gladdened Thy disciples with the promise of the Holy Spirit; and they were assured by the blessing that Thou art the Son of God, the Redeemer of the world."[52]

On the fiftieth day after Pascha Sunday and the tenth after the Ascension is celebrated the feast commemorating the Descent of the Holy Spirit upon the disciples of Christ. It is called the feast of the Pentecost and lasts for two days. The first day of this feast is sacred to the honor and glory of the Most Holy Trinity and the memory of the descent of the Holy Spirit, and is called "Trinity Day." The second day is celebrated in honor of the All-holy, life-giving, and All-mighty Spirit, and is called "Spirit-Day." The Church prepares for this feast by commemorating all the dead the day before. On Trinity Day, Vespers follows immediately after the Liturgy, and at this service three prayers are offered while kneeling, that the Lord may send down to us the grace of the Holy Spirit and remember all the departed souls. It is customary to decorate the churches and houses on this day with trees and flowers, and to stand at Vespers holding flowers. The trees and the flowers are offered to God as the first-fruits of summer, and remind us that Christians receive the renovation of their souls through the action of the Holy Spirit. In honor of this great feast, the Church dispenses from fasting on the Wednesday and Friday of the week following it.

Troparion for the day

Blessed art Thou, O Christ our God, Who hast shown forth the fishermen as supremely wise, by sending down upon them the Holy Spirit, and through them didst draw the world into Thy net. O Lover of mankind, glory be to Thee.[53]

The Sunday following that of the Pentecost is consecrated to all the Saints, especially to those in whose honor no special celebration has been instituted, on account of their numbers, or because of their names being unknown. With this day ends the series of movable services.

The Different Ministrations

Administering the Sacraments of Baptism and Chrismation

Baptism is the Sacrament whereby a person who believes in Christ, dies unto his or her former sinful life through immersion, thrice performed with the words: "The servant of God N. is baptized in the name of the Father and the Son and the Holy Spirit," and receives the grace of the Holy Spirit, which confers a renovated and holy life.

Chrismation is the Sacrament whereby the person who has received baptism receives the grace of the Holy Spirit through the anointing of the different parts of the body with holy chrism, with the words: "the seal of the gift of the Holy Spirit," confirming him or her in the renovated, Christian life. At present both sacraments are normally performed together, and form one church rite.

In view of the great importance of these two sacraments in the life of a Christian, they are preceded by certain sacred acts which prepare persons to receive them worthily, and are followed by other acts, impressing on the Christian the memory of their deep significance. To the former acts belong the rites of conferring a name, of doing reverence to the holy temple, and of reception among the catechumens. The latter acts include ablutions, tonsuring, and joining the Church.

PRAYER FOR A WOMAN WHO HATH GIVEN BIRTH TO A CHILD, AND NAMING THE CHILD

At the present time it is customary to administer the Sacrament of Baptism to a child soon after its birth. Therefore the Orthodox Church cares for the babes of Christian parents as for her children. As soon as a child is born in a Christian family, a priest is called and prays, in the name of the entire Church, "that the Lord may preserve the mother and new-born babe from all evil, shelter them under the shelter of His wings, forgive the mother's trespasses, raise her from the bed of sickness, and vouchsafe that her babe may do reverence to His holy temple." The priest recites this prayer wearing the Epitrachelion (stole).

In obedience to the statutes of the Church, the babe, on the eighth day after birth, is brought before the doors of the temple, whereby its parents signify their desire that it should also be a Christian. Here it is met by the priest, who blesses it (signs it) in the name of the Lord, gives it a Christian name, i.e., the name of some Saint, and prays to God "that the light of His countenance be signed upon it; that it be signed with the Cross of the only-begotten Son of God in its heart and understanding; that it may flee from the vanity of the world and every evil device of the Enemy and may keep God's commandments; and that the name of God may remain on it forever unrenounced." The babe is given a Christian name in token of its covenant with Christ, as a pledge that it may hope for salvation with the Saints, and as a reminder that it must emulate the life of the Saint whose name it bears. From this moment the babe enters the class of catechumens, i.e., of those who are preparing to receive holy baptism. In our country, the ceremony of naming is usually performed within the first days after birth, immediately after the prayer for the mother, and not before the door of a church, but at home, because the severity of the climate does not allow for carrying so young a babe out into the open air.

As the giving of a name is of great importance in a person's life, the day which is sacred to the memory of the Saint whose name he or she bears is called a person's "name's day," and, to that person, is a festive one, on which he or she asks the help of God and the Saint towards leading a life worthy of that name. Christians look at their Saints as on their guardian angels; hence, a person's "name's day" is also called his or her "angel's day."

PRAYER ON THE FORTIETH DAY AFTER BIRTH

In imitation of the Virgin who, on the fortieth day after the birth of the Infant Jesus, brought Him to the temple, to present Him to the Lord, every Christian mother should bring her babe to church on the fortieth day after birth. The priest meets them in the vestibule, blesses mother and child, and prays that the Lord may bless them, purify and sanctify the mother and hold her worthy to partake of the Holy Eucharist,[54] and the babe borne of her to receive the Sacrament of Baptism.

THE RITE OF RECEPTION AMONG THE CATECHUMENS

This rite is performed just before baptism. The candidate for baptism is conducted or carried into the vestibule of the temple and stands before the font, looking towards the East, ungirdled, bareheaded and barefooted, with hands hanging down.

By this ceremony he indicates that he desires to cast off the old man and don a new man, after the image of Christ; that he aspires from darkness unto light, of which the East is the symbol, and humbly awaits illumination from Christ. The priest breathes thrice in his face, blesses him and lays his hand upon his head. The priest's breath recalls the breath of life which the Creator breathed into the nostrils of the first created man, and betokens the breath of new life imparted through the Sacrament of Baptism. The blessing in the name of Christ betokens separation from the community of the unbelieving, and the imposition of the hand — the entry under the shelter of the Church. Laying his hand on the catechumen's head, the priest recites the preliminary prayer, in which he asks that the Lord may inscribe him in the Book of Life and receive him into His holy flock. This prayer is followed by the catechumen rites:

EXORCISM, THE RENUNCIATION OF THE DEVIL, THE DECLARATION OF THE DESIRE TO JOIN CHRIST, THE PROFESSION OF FAITH, AND THE WORSHIP OF THE HOLY TRINITY

In the exorcism the priest, in the name of the Almighty, commands the Devil to depart from the person who has been sealed with the name of the Lord Jesus Christ, and prays that God may expel the impure spirit from the catechumen and make him a member of His holy Church. At the words, "Expel from him every evil and impure spirit which hideth and maketh its lair in his heart," the priest blows on the mouth, brow and breast of the catechumen in token of the expulsion from his soul of all impurity.

After these prayers, the catechumen is turned with his face towards the West, which symbolizes darkness and evil, and to the thrice repeated question, uttered by the priest, "Dost thou renounce Satan and all his works, and all his angels, and all his service, and all his pomp?" he answers, with hands uplifted, "I do." Then the priest asks thrice, "Hast thou renounced Satan?" and he answers, "I have," and, at the priest's command, signifies, by blowing and spitting, his contempt of all things devilish.

Having renounced the devil, the catechumen turns again towards the East, with his hands down, and to the priest's question "Dost thou unite thyself unto Christ?" he answers, "I do." The priest again asks, "Hast thou united thyself unto Christ?" He answers, "I have." The priest then asks, "Dost thou believe in Him?," to which the catechumen answers, "I believe in Him as King and God," and forthwith recites the Creed. The last two questions the priest utters thrice, and each time receives an affirmative answer, which is followed each time by the Creed.

Having received the catechumen's renunciation of his former sinful life, the expression of his readiness to live with Christ and his profession of faith, the priest commands him, as a new member of the Kingdom of

Christ, "Bow down also before Him." The catechumen bows himself to the ground before the Holy Trinity, saying, "I bow down before the Father, and the Son, and the Holy Spirit, the Trinity one in essence and indivisible." The rite concludes with a prayer in which the priest asks the Lord to count the catechumen worthy to receive holy baptism.

The same rite is performed over adult candidates for baptism, and over infants. But as an infant cannot speak for itself, its sponsors answer for it. Both the catechumen rites and that of Baptism are performed for adult persons in a church, in the presence of the faithful. But in the case of infants, it is allowed to perform both at the parents' home, when the babe's weakness and the severity of the climate do not allow for taking it to church.

THE ORDER OF BAPTISM AND CHRISMATION

To perform the Sacrament of Baptism, the priest[55] puts on light-colored or white vestments, to express the joy of the Church at receiving a new member. Candles are lit around the edge of the font, the censer is swung, and the sponsors are given candles to hold. The lighted candles symbolize the spiritual illumination which is imparted through the Sacrament of Baptism, while the clouds of incense indicate the grace of the Holy Spirit, through whose operation man's regeneration takes place in this Sacrament.

The Order of Baptism consists of the consecration of the water, the anointing of the water and of the person baptized with consecrated oil, the immersion of the person into the water, the investing him with white garments, anointing with chrism or myrrh, the circumambulation of the font, and readings from the Holy Scriptures.

To the petitions of the Great Ectenia, with which the rite of Baptism begins, are added petitions, "That this water may be sanctified through the power and action and descent of the Holy Spirit... — That there may

be sent down into it the grace of redemption, the blessing of Jordan...
— That he may prove himself to be a son of light, and an heir of eternal
good things... — That he may be a member and partaker of the death
and resurrection of Christ our God..." The priest then offers a prayer,
"Wherefore, O King Who lovest mankind, come Thou now through the
descent of Thy Holy Spirit, and sanctify this water *(thrice)."* At the words
of the prayer, "Let all adverse powers be crushed beneath the sign of the
image of Thy Cross," he blesses the water thrice and blows upon it. By
this act he expresses his belief that the devil is expelled by the name of
Jesus Christ.

The water being consecrated, the priest proceeds to consecrate the
oil by prayer, in token of reconciliation, and while "Alleluia" is being
solemnly sung, he makes with the oil the sign of the Cross on the water.
Before this rite the admonition, "Let us attend!," is uttered, to draw to it
the attention of those present, and to signify that it conveys a mystical
meaning. As water, which once upon a time submerged the entire human
race, symbolizes purification, and oil gathered from the olive tree, a
branch of which was brought to Noah in the ark by the dove, in token
of reconciliation, symbolizes mercy, so the connection of both these
symbols signifies that the purification of man by the waters of baptism
takes place through the mercy of God.

Having thus prepared the material for the Sacrament, the priest now
proceeds to prepare for it the person about to receive it. He anoints
the brow, ears, breast, hands and feet with the consecrated oil, in token
that, through baptism, man, like unto a branch of the wild olive tree, is
grafted unto the good olive tree, which is Christ. As man dies in baptism
to his former life and comes forth a new man to battle with evil, so the
anointing with oil serves him, as one dead, as a preparation for burial
and, as a soldier of Christ as a preparation for the struggle with iniquity.

The act of baptism itself is performed by the thrice repeated immersion of the recipient of the Sacrament into the water, with the words, "The servant (or handmaid) of God N. is baptized in the name of the Father, Amen, and of the Son, Amen, and of the Holy Spirit, Amen." During the immersion he who is baptized is turned to the East. At this moment the grace of the Holy Spirit descends on him and gives him a new life, washing away all sins from his soul; while being immersed, he is entombed with Christ; when lifted out of the water, he rises with Him. The blessings which man receives in the Sacrament of Baptism are expressed in the words of the Psalm (31st) which is sung immediately after the immersion: "Blessed are they whose iniquities are forgiven, and whose sins are covered. Blessed is the man unto whom the Lord imputeth not sin ... Many are the scourges of the sinner, but mercy shall encircle him that hopeth in the Lord. Be glad in the Lord, and rejoice, ye righteous; and glory, all ye that are upright of heart."

In token of the purity of the neophyte's soul, the priest invests him with a white garment, calling it, "the robe of righteousness," and in token that he shall live after baptism, he places round his neck a Cross, the symbol of walking after Christ. During the robing, a troparion is sung, indicating the meaning of the white garment: "Grant unto me the robe of light, O Thou Who coverest Thyself with light as with a garment, O Christ our God, plenteous in mercy."

As special help from God is needed to follow after Christ and preserve the soul's purity obtained through baptism, the Sacrament of Chrismation is administered to the neophyte immediately after the robing. The priest makes the sign of the Cross with chrism on his brow, eyes, nostrils, lips, ears, breast, hands and feet, saying each time, "The seal of the gift of the Holy Spirit." Through this unction is imparted the grace of the Holy Spirit, which confirms the new life and gives the strength to live in Christ.

The priest now walks three times around the font with the neophyte and sponsors, to the chant: "As many as have been baptized into Christ, have put on Christ." The circumambulation of the font signifies the triumph and joy of the Church, because a Christian has been joined with Christ forever.

The order of the sacrament concludes with a reading from the Apostle, in which the meaning of baptism is set forth, also the benefits bestowed by this Sacrament, and the duties which it imposes on us, and with a reading from the Gospel, on the institution of the Sacrament by Jesus Christ.

THE SPONSORS

At every baptism whether of an adult or of an infant, sponsors are absolutely necessary. If the former, they serve as witnesses of the neophyte's profession of faith and the vows he takes; if the latter, they answer all questions for the infant. After baptism they assume the spiritual care of the neophyte and are bound to be his guides in Christian life and to see to his religious education. Through these duties a spiritual relationship is established between the sponsors and their god-child, and also the latter's parents; the sponsors are god-fathers and god-mothers. As the sponsors assume important responsibilities towards their godchildren, the Church rules that they shall have attained the age of discretion (the godfather to be not under 15, the godmother not under 13) that they shall be persons of good moral standing with a knowledge of the fundamental doctrines of the Orthodox Church and participate in the rite of baptism as "honorary persons," but in that case it is absolutely necessary that the god-father should be Orthodox if the neophyte is of the male sex, or the god-mother, if of the female sex. Parents may not be sponsors for their own children; nor may monks or nuns be sponsors.

THE RITES OF ABLUTION AND TONSURE

In ancient times neophytes did not lay aside their white garments for seven days, nor wash the spots on their bodies which had been anointed with holy chrism; and, that the seal laid on them by the unction might not be defaced, they wore wreaths or bandages. On the eighth day they came to church, and there the priest loosed the girdle of their garments, removed the bandage from their brow and washed the anointed parts. At present this ablution is performed immediately after the reading of the Gospel. The priest first prays, "O Thou Who, through holy baptism, hast given unto Thy servant N. remission of sins, and hast bestowed upon him a life of regeneration: Do Thou Thyself, O Master and Lord, be pleased to illumine his heart with the light of Thy countenance continually. Keep the shield of his faith unassailed by the enemy. Preserve pure and unpolluted the garment of incorruption wherewith Thou has covered him, upholding inviolate in him by Thy grace the seal of the Spirit, and showing mercy unto him and unto us, according to the multitude of Thy compassions. O Master, Lord our God, Who through the font bestowest heavenly Illumination upon them that are baptized, Who hast regenerated Thy newly-enlightened servant by water and the Spirit, and hast granted unto him remission of his sins, whether voluntary or involuntary: Lay Thine almighty hand upon him and preserve him by the power of Thy goodness. Maintain inviolate the pledge of the Spirit, and make him worthy of life eternal and of Thy favor." Then he sprinkles the neophyte with water, reminding him that, "Thou art justified, thou art illumined, thou art sanctified. Thou art washed in the name of our Lord Jesus Christ and of the Spirit of our God." After which, he wipes with a sponge the anointed parts of his body, reminding him that, "Thou art baptized. Thou art illumined. Thou hast been anointed with Chrism. Thou art sanctified. Thou art washed: in the name of the Father, and of the Son, and of the Holy Spirit. Amen."

Immediately after the ablution, the tonsure of the hair is performed. It was customary among the ancient Hebrews to shear the hair and burn it on the altar in token of entire self-consecration to God. This ancient custom passed into the Christian Church. Christians shear the hair of newborn infants in token that, having received baptism, they have become citizens of the Kingdom of God on earth, and have consecrated themselves to the service of God, before Whom they have promised to cut away from their souls sinful thoughts and passions. After the ablution, the priest performs the tonsure in the name of the Most Holy Trinity, praying that God may help the neophyte to become learned in His law and to live according to that law.

The Rite of Joining the Church

The neophyte has now the right to enter the church, to take part in all the prayers and to partake of the Holy Eucharist. The first time he comes to church, he does so with some solemnity and this act is called, "joining the Church," (i.e., "being admitted into the community of Christians.") The priest meets the neophyte at the entrance of the church, takes him or her on his arm and, after making the sign of the Cross before the main door, says: "The servant (or handmaid) of God N. is admitted to join the Church in the name of the Father, and the Son, and the Holy Spirit; now and ever and unto the ages of ages, amen." Then he leads or carries the neophyte into the church with the words, "He (or she) cometh into Thy house to worship toward Thy holy temple." Pausing in the middle of the church, he repeats the words of admission, and adds, "In the midst of the church shall he hymn Thee." Once again he repeats the words of admission before the royal gates, and, if the neophyte be of the male sex, leads or carries him into the sanctuary; if of the female sex, he brings her only as far as the royal gates, and repeats the prayer of St. Symeon, "Now lettest Thou Thy servant depart in peace, O Master...". Then he gives up the neophyte to the sponsors.

As infants, at the present day, are, usually baptized before the fortieth day after birth, the rite of their admission into the church usually takes place the fortieth day, when the mother brings her babe herself to present it to the Lord and to receive herself the permission to partake of Holy Communion. Formerly, a mother used to receive communion on that day and the child also receives it then for the first time. The latter custom prevails to this day.

The Sacrament of Baptism properly performed cannot be repeated; that of Chrismation can be repeated only for such persons as having renounced the faith of Christ and adopted paganism, Mohammedanism, or Judaism, etc., again return to Christ.

THE RITE OF ADMISSION INTO THE ORTHODOX CHURCH OF FOLLOWERS OF OTHER CHRISTIAN CONFESSIONS

Heterodox Christians are received into the Orthodox Church by Baptism and Chrismation, unless the bishop of the diocese chooses to exercise *economy*, in which case the person seeking admission confesses his sins before a priest, but does not receive absolution. Then, in the vestibule (or, where there is none, by the western entrance), he abjures all his former errors of faith and professes the doctrine of the Orthodox Church. The priest then conducts him into the church, saying: "Enter into the Church of God and cast away all wrongs and errors." He kneels in the middle of the church before a lectern, upon which lie a Cross and Gospel, and hears a prayer in which the priest beseeches the Lord to grant that this man may irrevocably, without deceit or guile, be joined unto the Holy Catholic Church. After this prayer he rises and pledges himself under oath: "Firmly to maintain and profess the Orthodox faith, with the help of God, whole and intact, to his last breath, and to fulfill all its obligations," and, in affirmation of this promise, kisses the Cross and Gospel. After taking the oath, he kneels once more, and the priest pronounces over him the prayer of remission and absolution, anoints him with the holy chrism and places a Cross around his neck. The rite concludes with the ectenia, in which the sponsors are prayed for, and then the dismissal.

The Rite of Anointing Tsars at Their Coronation

The Anointing of a Tsar is a sacred act by which the grace of the Holy Spirit is imparted to him, to fit him for the performance of the highest ministry on earth. The entire rite consists of two acts: the coronation, and the anointing with holy chrism. In Russia this rite is performed in Moscow, in the Church of the Dormition.

The order of the ceremonies is as follows: First a *moleben* is sung for the health of their Imperial Majesties, followed by the Office of the Hours. During this service, the imperial regalia are brought into the church—the purple mantle, the crown, the scepter and the orb.

THE EMPEROR'S CROWN

Bishops in full pontificals meet them, with incense, sprinkle them with holy water, and remain near the entrance, in readiness

THE EMPRESS' CROWN

to receive their Imperial Majesties. When the Emperor and Empress enter the church, one of the Metropolitans greets them and offers them the Cross to kiss while another sprinkles them with holy water. Their Majesties then proceed into the church (preceded by the bishops) perform a prostration before the royal gates, kiss the principal icons, then, ascending the dais, seat themselves on the thrones prepared for them in the middle of the church, while the bishops station themselves in two lines from the throne to the royal gates. During this time, Psalm 100 is sung, "Of mercy and judgment will I sing unto Thee, O Lord..."

When their Majesties have taken their seats, the presiding Metropolitan ascends the imperial dais and asks the Emperor what faith he professes. The Emperor replies by reciting the Creed in a loud voice.

After this public profession of faith by the Emperor, the rite of coronation begins. After the hymn, "O Heavenly King," has been sung, the Great Ectenia is recited with the addition of petitions for a prosperous reign. Then are sung the hymn, "God is the Lord..." and the troparion, "Save, O Lord, Thy people...", followed by a paremia and readings from the Gospel and Epistle. The paremia speaks of the Divine protection extended over the Tsar; the Epistle — of obedience to Kings; the Gospel— of the tribute to Cæsar. After the reading of the Gospel lesson, the Emperor is invested with the purple and the chain of the Order of the Apostle Andrew the First-called, presented by the Metropolitan, with the words, "In the name of the Father,

THE SCEPTER

and the Son, and the Holy Spirit." Having received the purple, the Emperor inclines his head, the Metropolitan signs it with the Cross, by laying his hands on it crosswise, and prays, "that the Lord may anoint the Tsar with the oil of gladness, invest him with strength, crown him with precious stones, grant him length of days, place in his right hand the scepter of salvation, seat him on the throne of righteousness, keep him under His shelter and establish his rule." After this prayer the Emperor takes the crown from the cushion presented by the Metropolitan and places it upon his head, while the Metropolitan again utters the words, "In the name of the Father, and the Son and the Holy Spirit." After the Emperor has assumed the crown, the Metropolitan explains the meaning of the coronation rite: "This visible and material adornment of thy head is to thee a manifest sign that the King of Glory, Christ, invisibly crowneth thee, the head of the throne of All the Russias." Then, from a cushion presented by the Metropolitan, the Emperor takes in his right hand the scepter and in his left the orb (a small globe, symbolizing the lands subject to him), while the Metropolitan again utters the words, "In the name of the Father, and the Son and the Holy Spirit." Then the

THE ORB

Metropolitan tells the Emperor the meaning of the scepter and orb, as follows: "God-crowned, God-given, God-adorned, most pious Autocrat and great Sovereign, Emperor of All the Russias! Receive the scepter and the orb, which are the visible signs of the autocratic power given thee from the Most High over thy people, that thou mayest rule them and order for them the welfare they desire." Having assumed the imperial regalia, the Emperor seats himself upon the throne, and, laying the scepter and orb on a cushion presented to him by dignitaries, calls to him Her Majesty the Empress. Her Majesty rises from her throne and kneels before the Emperor, who takes the crown from

THE IMPERIAL PURPLE

his head and touches with it the Empress' head, then replaces the crown on his own head and places on hers a smaller crown, presented by a dignitary. Then the Empress is invested with the purple and the chain of St. Andrew, and seats herself on her throne. A deacon proclaims, "length of days to their Majesties" (as at the service of the Royal Hours), after which the Emperor kneels down and, in a loud voice, offers a prayer in which he beseeches the Lord as follows: "Instruct me in the Work on which Thou hast sent me, grant me wisdom and direct me for this great ministry." The rite of coronation concludes with a prayer offered by the Metropolitan, all present kneeling and with the singing of the hymn, "We praise Thee, O God." After this hymn the Liturgy begins.

It is during the Liturgy that the rite of anointing takes place. As the Liturgy begins, the Emperor puts away the crown. After the Gospel lesson, the Gospel is presented to their Majesties to kiss. When the communion hymn has been sung, the Emperor gives his sword to a dignitary, and walks, mantled, to the royal gates, which, at this moment are thrown open. The Empress follows him and stops midway between the throne and the ambo.

Two Metropolitans step out of the Sanctuary. The presiding Metropolitan anoints the Emperor with holy chrism on the brow, the eyes, the nostrils, the lips, the ears, the breast, and the hands—palm and back—saying every time, "the seal of the gift of the Holy Spirit"; the other Metropolitan wipes off the chrism with cotton. Then the Emperor steps aside and stands at the right side of the royal gates, next to the icon of the Saviour. The Empress now approaches the royal gates, and the presiding Metropolitan anoints her with holy chrism, on the brow only, with the words, "the seal of the gift of the Holy Spirit;" then the Empress steps aside and stands at the left side of the royal gates, next to the icon of the Mother of God.

THE IMPERIAL
SWORD

After the rite of anointing has been performed, their Majesties receive holy communion. The Metropolitan conducts the Emperor, through the royal gates, into the Sanctuary, and there, at the altar, gives him the Eucharist, as to the Anointed of God and the supreme protector of the Christian Church, after the rite for the clergy, i.e., he places in his hand a portion of the Body of Christ, then lets him partake of the Blood of Christ from the chalice. The Empress receives communion in the usual manner before the royal gates. After receiving communion, their Imperial Majesties resume their seats on the thrones, where, after the prayers of thanksgiving and for length of days have been said, they receive the loyal congratulations of churchmen and laymen.

The Order
of the Consecration
# of a Church

The material church is the visible image of the spiritual body called, "the Church of Christ," the Head of which is Christ, and the members are all who believe in Christ. Therefore, as every human being enters into the Church through the Sacraments of Baptism and Confirmation, so every new church becomes a House of God, for the dispensing within its walls of the gifts of the grace of the Holy Spirit, only after it has been consecrated by means of certain sacred offices, which bear some similitude to the Sacraments of Baptism and Confirmation.

RITE AT THE LAYING OF THE FOUNDATION OF A CHURCH.
This rite is performed at the laying of the foundation, and consists of the placing of the foundation stone. The bishop, or a priest deputed by him, comes with Cross and icons to the spot dug for the foundation. The service begins with a *moleben* and consecration of water; then, to the singing of appropriate troparia in honor of the person in whose name the church is to be built, the bishop or priest censes around the spot and offers a prayer, wherein he asks that, "the Lord may keep the builders of the temple unharmed and the foundations thereof unimpaired, and that He may help the completion thereof unto the glory of God." After this prayer he takes a square-cut stone (a cube), on which is engraved a Cross (and under the Cross is a hollow place to hold sacred relics), sprinkles the stone with holy water, and having made with it the sign of the Cross, places it in the foundation with the words: "The Most High hath founded this church; God is in the midst of her, she shall not be shaken; God shall

help her right early in the morning." Upon the stone is laid a metallic plate with an inscription, setting forth in whose honor the church is founded, and giving the names of the reigning Emperor, the local bishop, and the persons at whose expense the church is to be built, and also the name of the Saint whose relics, if any, are deposited in the foundation.

After this ceremony, the bishop or priest plants a wooden Cross on the spot where the altar is to stand, with a prayer, "that the Lord may bless and sanctify this spot by the force and operation of the precious and life-giving tree of the Cross." On the Cross there also is an inscription, setting forth in whose name the altar is consecrated, under the reign of what Emperor, and with what bishop's blessing, also in what year, month and date the foundation was laid.

THE RITE OF THE CONSECRATION OF A CHURCH

On the eve of the consecration of a newly-built church, an All-night Vigil is celebrated before the sanctuary, with the royal gates closed.

The consecration itself is performed in different ways, according to who the consecrator is—a bishop, or a priest deputed by a bishop.

CONSECRATION BY A BISHOP

The following preparations for the consecration are made: Before the royal gates, upon a table covered with a white linen cloth, are placed: a Gospel, a Cross, the sacred vessels, the spoon, the spear, the veils, the aërs, the cloths with which the Altar and the Table of Oblations are to be dressed, a rope for fastening the altar, and nails. Around this table are placed four candlesticks. In the Sanctuary near the Bema are placed upon a separate table; the holy chrism, rose water, the twig for anointing with chrism, an aspergilla, and some stones. Before the icon of the Saviour in the screen (*ikonostas*), upon a lectern, are placed the sacred relics, on a paten, covered with the asterisk and aër.

On the day of consecration, the sacred relics are transferred to the nearest church and there placed upon the altar. If there is no church near enough, they remain where they are, before the icon of the Saviour.

The rite of consecration begins with a *moleben* with consecration of water, after which the celebrants put on full vestments, and, over them, a wide and long apron, tied round the neck and waist, and under the arms, and then carry the table with the church belongings into the Sanctuary; this done, the royal gates are closed.

When the royal gates are closed and all persons who are not participants in the ceremony have gone out of the sanctuary, the Altar is established thusly, the bishop sprinkles with holy water the props of the Altar, then pours into the hollows prepared for the nails some cero-mastix (a preparation of wax mixed with sundry fragrant and adhesive substances, incense and white sulfur), and sprinkles the top board of the altar, the nails and stones. Thereupon the priests lay the top board upon the props and hammer in the nails with the stones. During all these proceedings psalms are sung. When the Altar is established, the royal gates are opened, and the bishop, kneeling, offers a prayer that the Lord may send down the Holy Spirit and sanctify the temple and altar. He then re-enters the sanctuary and the royal gates are closed once more.

Then begins the ablution of the altar. To the singing of psalms, the bishop rubs the board with soap in the form of a Cross, and pours upon it tepid water, which has been sanctified by prayer, when the priests take cloths and rub the altar dry. Then he takes red wine mixed with rose water, pours the mixture upon the altar in the shape of a Cross and rubs it in, wherein he is assisted by the priests. With the same wine he sprinkles the Antimins prepared for the new church. The priests take sponges sprinkled with holy water and wipe off the altar. This ceremony of ablution is symbolical of the altar's high significance. The tepid water symbolizes the grace of the Holy Spirit, which warms the hearts of the faithful; the rose water recalls the precious myrrh brought by the women for Christ's entombing while the red wine signifies the Blood of Christ, shed for our salvation.

After the ablution, the bishop anoints with holy chrism the top board and the props, as also the Antimins prepared for the Altar. Then begins the vesting of the Altar: first in a white cover, which is tied to the Altar cross-wise, with the rope; over this first cover a second one is slipped of a brilliant material (it is called *endyton*, i.e., "covering," "garment"—a Greek word); then on the altar is laid the *eilyton* ("wrap," also a Greek word), and in that the Antimins is enfolded. All these articles are put in place after having been sprinkled with holy water, to the chanting of a psalm. This completes the consecration of the altar, after which the bishop and priest put away the aprons, and the royal gates are opened.

The bishop now proceeds to the consecration of the church. Preceded by candle-bearers, while a psalm is chanted, he walks around the whole church, censing it as he goes; two priests follow him: one sprinkles the wall with holy water; and the other anoints with chrism the wall above the Bema, above the western door, and the northern and southern wall above the doors and windows. Reentering the Sanctuary, the bishop lights a light on the Bema; from this all the candles and lamps are lit.

After the consecration, the bishop goes in procession, while troparia are chanted in honor of the martyrs, to the nearest church, to bring thence the holy relics.[56] There, approaching the altar, upon which the relics are reposing, he prays, kneeling, that the Lord, hearing the holy martyrs' prayers, may grant us a share in His inheritance; then he censes the holy relics, takes the paten containing them upon his head, and, thus carrying them, returns in procession to the newly built church and walks around it on the outside, to the singing of troparia on the upbuilding and establishing of the Church of the Saviour, at the same time sprinkling the external walls with holy water. Then he stops before the western entrance, places the paten with the relics on a lectern, and blesses his assistant celebrants. Thereupon the choir enters the church and the doors are closed after them. The processional circumambulation of the church signifies that the building is consecrated to God forever.

Standing before the closed door of the church, the bishop calls out, "Lift up your heads, O ye gates; and be ye lifted up, ye everlasting doors; and the King of Glory shall enter in." The choir, from within the church, sing in reply, "Who is this King of Glory?" While these words are sung, the bishop censes the relics. Then he calls out again, "Lift up your heads, O ye gates; and be ye lifted up, ye everlasting doors; and the King of Glory shall enter in." Again, the choir reply from within the church, "Who is this King of Glory?" The bishop here offers a prayer, "that the Lord may stablish the newly built temple and let it endure unto the end of time." Then he takes up the paten with the holy relics, and, making with it the sign of the Cross before the entrance, calls out, "The Lord of hosts, He is the King of Glory." These words are repeated by the choir within the church. At this moment, the doors are thrown open, and the bishop enters in procession, bearing the paten with the relics on his head, places it on the altar, anoints a particle of the relics with chrism, places it in a small casket which he fills with cero-mastix, and which a priest, having taken it from him, and closed down the lid, deposits inside the central prop of the altar; the other particle of the holy relics the bishop deposits in the Antimins, after having also anointed it with chrism. When the holy relics have been deposited in their places, a prayer is offered for the builders of the church and dismissal of the consecration is made, after which follow the Hours and the Liturgy.

THE RITE OF THE CONSECRATION OF A CHURCH BY A PRIEST

The special features of the consecration of a church when performed by a priest are the following: (1) it is not a paten with holy relics which is placed on a lectern before the icon of the Saviour, but an Antimins, consecrated beforehand by a bishop and containing holy relics; (2)

at the establishing of the Altar, the prescribed psalms are sung, but no prayer is offered, as that was offered by the bishop at the consecration of the Antimins; (3) at the ablution of the Altar, it is not washed with red wine and rosewater, as this act was performed by the bishop with the Antimins; (4) the Altar is fastened with the rope not crosswise, but in the usual way; (5) the walls are not anointed with chrism; (6) it is the Antimins which is carried in procession around the church; (7) no holy relics are placed inside the prop under the Altar.

The Rite of Confession

When a Christian falls into sin after baptism, he violates the vows he took at baptism, separates himself from the Church, and forfeits the right to partake of holy communion. But there remains to him the possibility of cleansing himself again from sins and being saved; for Jesus Christ gave to His disciples the power of remitting the sins of those who repented and of again joining them to His Church. This power the Apostles transmitted to their successors, the bishops, and these again empowered the priests to hear the repentant confessions of the faithful and to remit their sins in the name of Jesus Christ, if they judged that their repentance was sincere and strong. This remission of sins is given in the Sacrament of Penance which is therefore called a "second baptism," a "baptism by tears," and the office in which it is performed is called the "Rite of Confession."

The Sacrament of Penance is one in which the Christian who confesses his sins before the entire Church or her representative, and asks for pardon, receives absolution from the priest, and at the same moment is invisibly absolved by Christ Himself. Hence, the rite of Confession consists of three acts: prayers for the remission of sins; confession of sins before the priest; and absolution from sins in the name of Jesus Christ.

After hearing the preliminary prayers, the penitential troparia, the Penitential Psalm and the prayers for the remission of sins, the penitent, standing before the icon of the Saviour, confesses his sins to the priest, concealing nothing, adducing no excuses to minimize his transgressions, then asks for pardon and absolution. After confession, he kneels and bows his head. The priest then prays that the Lord may forgive the penitent's sins and join him to His holy Church, covers his head with the Epitrachelion (stole) in token that he, the priest—through the grace of

God—has the power to remit sins in the name of Jesus Christ; blesses him, and utters the words of absolution: "Our Lord and God, Jesus Christ,by His grace and the bountifulness of His lovingkindness, forgive thee, child, N., all thy transgressions; and I, an unworthy priest, by His power which is given unto me, forgive thee and absolve thee from all thy sins, in the name of the Father, and the Son, and the Holy Spirit, Amen." With these words the grace of the Holy Spirit descends into the soul of the penitent and cleanses it of sins, so that he, by the grace of God, goes from the presence of the priest a pure and holy man.

As only he receives remission of sins who, repenting of them, profoundly regrets having committed them and firmly determines to abstain from them in the future, such repentance necessitates a period of preparation. During this time the Christian lays aside all worldly pre-occupations, and devotes himself to fasting, prayer, meditation on his soul, and, the better to do all this, seeks solitude and keeps away from all amusements and distracting things. The length of the time of preparation depends on how long a time a man can spare from his worldly obligations.

The priest who receives a penitent's confession enters into a close spiritual connection with him, and therefore is called his "spiritual father," while the penitent is the priest's "spiritual child." The spiritual father does not merely hear the sinner's confession, and judge the condition of his soul; he, like a physician, tries to find out what is his spiritual disease, points out to the careless transgressor how important and deep-seated his sins are, and him who despairs of his improvement and salvation he supports and encourages by hope in the mercy of God. This means that the better the spiritual father knows his spiritual children, the more useful his counsels and instructions will be to them. It is a rule, therefore, that a spiritual father shall not be changed without absolute necessity.

It sometimes happens that a spiritual father remits a penitent's sins on condition that he will fulfill some task or discipline imposed upon him, either of prohibition or command; this is called a "penance." The spiritual father imposes a penance to help the penitent to break himself of a sinful habit, or to cure him of carelessness with regard to his self-correction, or again to calm his conscience troubled by sin and not let him sink into despair. The penance imposed by one spiritual father cannot be remitted by another, excepting in case of the penitent's dangerous illness or that of the death of the spiritual father himself.

The Rite of the Sacrament of Orders

The Sacrament of Orders is that in which one who has been canonically selected and ordained by a bishop receives the grace of the Holy Spirit and is instituted to perform the Sacraments and tend the flock of Christ, i.e., to govern a Christian church. As the grace of the Holy Spirit is imparted in this Sacrament through the imposition of the bishop's hands, the act of performing the sacrament is named the *Cheirotony*, which means in Greek, the "stretching out" or "laying on of hands." The rite is the same for all grades of priesthood—that of bishop, presbyter, or deacon, differing only in that it is performed at different moments of the Liturgy. It consists of the following acts: presentation of the person selected for holy orders, circumambulation of the altar, the prayer of consecration, the laying on of hands, and vesting with the sacred vestments.

The Ordination of a Deacon

As the deacon does not perform the Sacrament of the Eucharist, but only ministers thereat, his ordination takes place after the consecration of the Holy Gifts. Two sub-deacons conduct the deacon-elect from the middle of the church before the bishop, who is seated on a throne at the left of the altar, and the deacons utter the words: "Command, command, command, holy Master." The first "command" is addressed to the people, the second to the clergy, the third to the bishop. This indicates that in ancient times the people and clergy as well as the bishop took part in the election of persons to be ordained for sacred functions. The deacon-elect bows himself to the ground before the bishop and receives his blessing. Then the deacons lead him thrice around the Altar in token that he vows to devote himself forever to the service of the church. During this act, he kisses the corners of the altar in token of reverence for God, after each circumambulation bows himself to the ground before the bishop, and kisses his hand and Thigh-shield (*palitsa*) in token of submissiveness to his authority. All through this ceremony are sung the following sacred hymns: "O ye holy martyrs, who valiantly contended and received the crown, pray to the Lord that our souls may be saved." — "Glory to Thee, Christ God, the Apostles' boast and the martyrs' joy, who preached the consubstantial Trinity." — "Rejoice, O Isaiah! the Virgin is with child and bringeth forth a son, Emmanuel, God and man, the Orient is His name, whom magnifying, we call the Virgin blessed."[57] After the circumambulation, the deacon-elect kneels down before the altar, but on only the right knee, because he does not receive the full ordination of priesthood, and lays his hands and forehead upon the altar, in token of consecration to God of all his faculties. Then the bishop, rising from the throne, covers the candidate's head with the ends of his Omophorion, blesses him, lays his hand upon his head, and speaks the prayer of ordination: "The Divine grace, which ever healeth what is infirm and supplieth what is wanting, passing through my hand, ordaineth this most pious subdeacon for deacon; let us therefore pray for him, that the grace of the All-holy Spirit may come upon him." The assistant celebrants in the Sanctuary sing thrice, "Lord have mercy!" and the choir responds *Kyrie eleison* ("Lord have mercy," in Greek), to indicate that our Russian Church received the *cheirotony* of priesthood from the Greek Church, and to this day preserves intact the bond that unites them. During the prayer of ordination, the recipient of the Sacrament receives the grace of the Holy Spirit, which ordaineth him for a sacred ministry. After the laying on of hands, the bishop delivers to the newly ordained deacon the vestments and signs of his office: the Orarion, the cuffs, and the fan, uttering the Greek word *Axios* ("worthy") which is repeated by the choir in the name of the people and clergy. Having received the fan, the newly ordained deacon takes his stand at the left side of the Altar and fans the Holy Gifts, calling to mind as he does so that he must minister at the Altar of God with the same reverence with which the holy angels minister to God Himself. At the same Liturgy, the newly ordained deacon receives communion and recites the Ectenia of Thanksgiving at the close of the Liturgy.

The Ordination of a Presbyter (Priest)

The deacon who is to be ordained priest is led out by deacons into the middle of the church, before the bishop, after the singing of the Cherubic Hymn, in order that he may on the same day take part in the celebration of the Eucharist. The circumambulation of the altar is conducted by a priest. The candidate bends both knees before the altar, in token that he takes upon himself the greater ministry, and for that end is to receive the highest gift of priesthood. After the prayer of ordination, the bishop gives to the newly ordained priest the vestments of his office: the Epitrachelion (stole), the belt (zone), and the Phelonion (cope) and places in his hands the Clergy Service Book (manual of church services). The newly ordained priest then takes part in the further celebration of the Liturgy. After the consecration of the Holy Gifts, the bishop presents to him a portion of the Lamb, with the words, "Receive this pledge and preserve it whole and intact unto thy last breath, for thou shalt be held to account for it at the second and dread coming of our Lord God and Saviour, Jesus Christ." This ceremony indicates that the priest is the performer of the Holy Sacraments and that it is his duty to guard their sacredness, admitting to participate in them only them that are worthy. Before the exclamation, "Holy things for the holy," this pledge is returned to the bishop. The newly ordained priest then receives holy communion and reads the prayer for which the celebrant descends from the ambo.

The Consecration of a Bishop

The consecration of a bishop takes place at the beginning of the Liturgy, since a bishop has the right not only to perform the Sacrament of the Eucharist, but also to ordain deacons and priests; moreover it is performed not by one bishop but by several, i.e., by a convention of bishops. Before the beginning of the Liturgy, an archpriest and a deacon conduct the candidate to an ambo (or platform) placed in the middle of the church, where the bishops are seated. Here, standing on an *Orlets* (eagle-rug),[58] he recites the Creed, expounds in detail the doctrine of the properties of the Persons of the Holy Trinity and of the Incarnation of the Son of God, then pledges himself to observe the canons of the Apostles and Councils, the traditions of the Church, and to obey the Holy Synod of Bishops, and, lastly, takes an oath instituted for spiritual authorities, of fulfilling their duties in all conscience and the fear of God. Having taken the oath, he receives the blessing of the senior bishop present, and kisses the hands of the other bishops who are to consecrate him.

After the introit with the Gospel, the archpriest and deacon conduct the bishop-elect before the royal gates. Here he is met by the bishops and kneels before the altar on both knees. The bishops lay an open Gospel, text downward, upon his head, as though it were the hand of Christ Saviour, and hold it there. During this time the senior bishop says the prayer of consecration; after which the bishops chant "Lord have mercy," and lay their right hands upon the head of the bishop-elect.

This ends the consecration, and the new bishop is forthwith robed in the Saccos and Omophorion, during which act the word *"Axios"* is uttered loudly. Then he takes part in the celebration of the Liturgy. When the Liturgy is ended, the oldest of the bishops presents the newly consecrated bishop with the crosier. This is done on the ambo in the middle of the church.

THE CONSECRATION OF READERS AND ACOLYTES

These persons, when they enter the service of the Church, do not receive holy orders, but only a bishop's blessing. The bishop lays his hands on their heads, but does not pray for the grace of the Holy Spirit. The imposition of hands is not called *cheirotony*, but *cheirothesis* (tonsure). It usually takes place after the robing of the bishop, before the reading of the Hours. The bishop blesses the person chosen for reader or acolyte, lays his hand upon his head, and says a prayer, in which he asks God to help him to perform his ministry worthily, then tonsures him in the shape of a Cross in the name of the Father and the Son and the Holy Spirit. After this he puts on a short phelonion, and is given the book of the Apostle, from which he reads a few lines. Then the phelonion is taken from him; he puts on a sticharion (tunic) and is given a candlestick which he holds, standing through the Liturgy. The book and the candlestick are given him as insignia of his ministry.

When a reader is consecrated for sub-deacon, the bishop girds him over the sticharion with an orarion and, laying his hands on him, says a prayer, after which the newly consecrated sub-deacon receives a towel and basin, in token of his ministry to the bishop during divine service, and as an indication that his chief duty is to look after the cleanliness of the altar and the table of oblations.

PROMOTION

The Promotion to a higher rank in the hierarchy of an archdeacon, an archpriest, an hegumen (abbot of a monastery), and an archimandrite takes place during the Liturgy, just before the entry with the Gospel, The candidate for promotion is conducted to the ambo in the middle of the church, where the bishop is at the time. The bishop blesses him, prays that the Lord may "clothe him with grace, adorn him with righteousness, and grant that he may be a good example unto the others"; then, blessing him again, announces to which grade he promotes him and calls out, "Axios!" An abbot and an archimandrite are presented with a pastoral staff, and the archimandrite is, besides, invested with the miter and the pectoral Cross.

The Order of the Sacrament of Matrimony

Matrimony is the Sacrament in which, in the image of the union of Christ with the Church, the conjugal union between a man and woman is blessed, which means that the grace of a love as perfect as that which unites Christ and His Church is invoked on them for the blessed bearing and Christian rearing of children.

As matrimony can be entered into only by the mutual spontaneous consent of both the parties, and they must receive the blessing of the Church on their conjugal life, the order of the Sacrament of Matrimony consists of two rites—that of betrothal,[59] and that of marriage. In the former, the man and the woman affirm their mutual engagement before God and the Church; the rings are the pledge of that engagement. In the rite of marriage, their union is blessed with prayers, invoking upon them the grace of the Holy Spirit; of that grace the crowns are the visible token. In ancient times it was allowed to perform the rite of betrothal apart from that of marriage. In our day the latter is performed immediately after the former. Both these rites must be performed in a church, in the presence of witnesses, and on certain days prescribed by the canons.

The Rite of Betrothal

The priest, preceded by a candle bearer, comes out of the sanctuary through the royal gates holding in his hands the Cross and Gospel, which he lays on a table in the middle of the church. Then he approaches the main entrance of the church, where the bride and groom already stand (the former at the groom's left side), blesses them thrice with two lighted candles, which he then hands to them, conducts them into the church, walking before them and swinging the censer — the censing is expressly prescribed — and places them before the table, at a little distance from it. The betrothal begins with the Great Ectenia and two brief prayers, with the addition of special petitions: for the salvation of the betrothed couple, the granting them of children and peaceful mutual affection, for their abiding in harmony, firm in the faith, and for a blessing on them, that they may lead a blameless life. The prayers contain petitions for a blessing on the betrothed and on the betrothal. Then follows the ceremony of betrothal. The priest takes from the altar the rings which he received from the bride and groom before the beginning of the service. With the golden ring he makes the sign of the Cross thrice above the groom's head, with the words, "The servant of God N. is betrothed to the handmaid of God N. in the name of the Father, and the Son, and the Holy Spirit." This he repeats thrice, then slips the ring on the fourth finger (next to the little finger) of the groom's right hand. The same proceeding is repeated with the bride's silver ring. After the betrothal, it is prescribed by the canons of the Church that the sponsor, or, as is now the established custom, the groom's best man, shall change the rings thrice from one to the other, so that the bride's silver ring remains with the groom, and the groom's golden ring remains with the bride. The rings are given them in token of the life-long union into which they are entering.* The more precious metal of the groom's ring indicates his domination, while the exchange of rings between the bride and groom indicates that they engage to share all the toils and hardships of life, he not allowing himself to be uplifted by his supremacy, she not taking advantage of her weakness. That this exchange is made by the sponsor, generally selected among the elder relatives, indicates the consent of the family. The rite of betrothal ends with the priest praying that the Lord may establish these espousals in the faith, in harmony, in truth and love, and may bless from Heaven through the putting on of rings.

*In ancient times rings were used as seals, with which to seal storerooms in houses; so the possession of the master's ring gave power in the household. Consequently the exchange of rings meant mutual support, and common power over the household.

The Rite of Marriage

After the rite of betrothal, the bride and groom approach nearer to the lectern, holding the lighted candles, and again preceded by the censing priest. This serves to remind them that they must live their lives in conformity with the commandments of the Lord, which the priest proclaims, that their good deeds must shine in the world, and rise to Heaven like incense. As they approach, Psalm 127 is sung, in which are depicted the blessings which God sends to pious consorts: "Blessed are all they that fear the Lord, that walk in His ways. Thou shalt eat the fruit of thy labors; blessed art thou, and well shall it be with thee. Thy wife shall be as a fruitful vine on the sides of thy house, thy sons like young olive trees round about thy table. Behold, so shall the man be blessed that feareth the Lord. The Lord bless thee out of Sion, and mayest thou see the good things of Jerusalem all the days of thy life. And mayest thou see thy children's children; peace be upon Israel." This psalm is sung with the refrain after each verse: "Glory to Thee, our God, glory to Thee." The betrothed couple, in token of festivity, then take their stand on a rug. The priest now asks them, each separately, whether they have the spontaneous wish and firm intention to contract the conjugal union with each other, and whether they have not promised to contract that union with any one else. On receiving their affirmative answer to the former question and their negative to the second, the priest proceeds to the actual rite of marriage.

This rite begins with blessing the Kingdom of the Most Holy Trinity and with the Great Ectenia. To this ectenia are added petitions on behalf of the new spouses: that they be granted a blessing upon their marriage, chastity, well-favored children and joy in them, and a blameless life. Then the priest says three prayers, in which he asks that the Lord may grant to the couple a peaceful life, length of days, chastity, mutual love, long life to their children, grace in their offspring, an unfading crown of glory in the heavens, and an abundance of the good things of the earth so that they may be enabled to assist the needy; that the Lord may help the wife to obey her husband, and the husband to be the head of his wife; that He may remember also the parents who reared them, as parents' prayers make firm the foundations of houses. After these prayers the priest places a crown on the head of the groom, repeating thrice the words, "The servant of God N. is crowned for the handmaid of God N. in the name of the Father and the Son and the Holy Spirit." This he repeats, placing the other crown on the head of the bride, after which he blesses them thrice, saying, "O Lord, our God, with glory and honor crown them." The crowns symbolize their victory over their passions, as also the honor paid them for the chastity of their life before marriage, and reminds them that they must guard the purity of their lives after marriage also. In Greece they use wreaths of myrtle and olive branches. We in Russia use crowns in the shape of imperial ones, ornamented with images of the Saviour and His Mother. This indicates that the newly wedded spouses are to become the progenitors (*Knyáz*, i.e., "prince" and "princess," in the old language), of a new generation.

After the ceremony of marriage and the blessing, a prokimenon is sung, in which the essence of the Sacrament of Matrimony is set forth: "Thou hast set upon their heads crowns of precious stones; they asked life of Thee, and Thou gavest it them," after which readings from the Gospel and the Epistles are read. The Apostle lesson speaks of the importance of the Sacrament of Matrimony and of the mutual duties of the newly-wed; the Gospel tells of Christ's presence at the marriage at Cana in Galilee.

The readings are followed by the Triple Ectenia and the Ectenia of Supplication, ending with the chanting of the Lord's Prayer; then a cup with wine is brought. The priest blesses the cup, and presents it alternately to the husband and the wife to drink from, three times to each. This common cup signifies that they must live in an indissoluble union and share with each other joy and sorrow. The priest takes them by the hand and leads them three times around the lectern, while the sponsors (or, in Russia, the best men) follow, holding the crowns above their heads. During this circumambulation the same hymns are sung as at an ordination. The *first* hymn celebrates the Incarnation of Emmanuel and praises the Mother of God. In the *second* the crowned martyrs are besought to pray for the salvation of our souls, as a warning to the newly-espoused that they should walk through life in holiness and courageously overcome all temptations and allurements. The *third* hymn glorifies Christ, the Apostles' boast and the Martyrs' joy, at the same time also indicating to the newly-espoused that Christ should be their glory and joy in times of affliction, such as they are sure to encounter and share together in the course of their lives. This ceremony is symbolical of the solemnity and indissolubility of the conjugal union.

The priest now takes the crowns from the newly married couple, and addresses to each words of greeting and good wishes. To the husband he says, "Be thou magnified, O bridegroom, like unto Abraham, and be thou blessed like unto Isaac, and do thou multiply like unto Jacob, walking in peace, and keeping the commandments of God in righteousness." To the bride he says as he takes off her crown, "And thou, O bride: Be thou exalted like unto Sarah, and exult thou, like unto Rebecca, and do thou multiply, like unto Rachel. Rejoice thou in thy husband, fulfilling the conditions of the law, for so it is well-pleasing unto God." The couple, after the crowns have been removed, bow their heads at the priest's invitation, listen to his wishes of prosperity and give each other the kiss of love.

In ancient times newly wedded couples used to wear wreaths of myrtle or olive branches for the space of seven days, and on the eighth, removed them in church in the presence of the priest, who prayed to God to preserve their union inviolate. In our day this prayer is said immediately after the ceremony, before dismissal.

Conditions of the Legality of a Marriage

Besides the mutual consent of the parties, the following conditions must be observed for a marriage to be legal: (1) they must be of the legal age — the groom not less then 18, the bride not less than 16; (2) they must not be closely related. The forbidden relationship extends to the fourth degree, i.e., first cousins may not marry each other, nor may two brothers marry two sisters; within the fifth degree (the father's or mother's first cousin), and the sixth (second cousins), marriage is sometimes permitted, but not without a dispensation from the bishop; (3) both parties must be of sane mind, and (4) they must have authority to marry: if minors, from parents or guardians; if employed in military or civil service, from their superiors; if members of a commune, from the elder. In order to find out whether there are any obstacles to the projected marriage, the bans are published in the couple's parish church for three consecutive Sundays. In addition to this, information is procured concerning their age, their families, their religion, their marital status, widowed, have they been married once or more than once, and lastly, whether they have the necessary authority from parents, guardians, or superiors. All this information is entered into a book; the entry is then signed by the groom and bride, and by witnesses who certify the truth of the information and engage, in case their testimony should be proved false, to answer before the laws, civil and ecclesiastical. This is called the "record," and not until it is completed and signed, can the marriage ceremonies be performed.

The Order for a Second Marriage

The Orthodox Church allows widowers and widows, and also persons whose marriage has been dissolved for one of the legitimate reasons, to contract a second (and, occasionally, a third) marriage; but this she considers as a condescension to human weakness, and therefore the celebration of a second or third marriage does not take place with the same solemnity as that of a first marriage. The prayers at the rites of betrothal are omitted, and those that accompany the rite of marriage are of a penitential nature; the solemn entrance of the bridal pair to the singing of the 127th Psalm is also omitted. In ancient times crowns were not used. It is customary in our day to limit these curtailed rites to the cases when both parties have been married before. Where one of the two is contracting a first marriage, the rites are not curtailed.

The Sacrament of Holy Unction

Holy Unction is the Sacrament in the administration of which a sick person is anointed with holy oil, while the grace of the Holy Spirit is invoked on him, which healeth sickness, both bodily and spiritual. The oil for this Sacrament is consecrated by prayer, and it should be, according to the canons of the Church, performed by seven priests; but in case of need, one priest suffices.

A dish with wheat is placed upon a table. Into the midst of the wheat is placed a vessel containing oil and red wine, and around the dish are positioned seven candles and seven bodkins or twigs like those used in the rites of baptism and chrismation, wrapped around with cotton. Upon the same table are placed a Cross and Gospel. The grains of wheat symbolize resurrection and regeneration;[60] the oil—healing by the grace of God; and the red wine, mixed with the oil, indicate that the grace of God is given us for Christ's sake, who shed His blood on the Cross for our salvation. The seven candles symbolize the seven gifts of the Holy Spirit. During the performance of the sacramental rites, the patient (if he be able) and the bystanders hold in their hands lighted candles.

The service begins with the singing of a prayer for the healing of the patient. It consists principally of a canon which is sung with the refrain, "O Lord of many mercies, heal thy suffering servant N." Then the Great Ectenia is recited, with added petitions for the blessing of the oil by the descent of the Holy Spirit, and for the granting to the sufferer of the grace of the Holy Spirit. After this the priest prays, "that the Lord may sanctify this oil, so that it may be to those anointed with it for healing and deliverance from all passion, all defilement of flesh and spirit and from all evil."

The consecration of the oil is followed by the reading of seven Epistle readings, seven Gospel readings, the Triple Ectenia, seven times repeated, seven prayers for the healing of the sick man and the remission of his sins, lastly anointment of his body with the consecrated oil. After each reading from the Epistle and from the Gospel, and the ectenia, one of the priests, with a prayer for the recovery of the patient, takes up one of the bodkins, dips it in the oil and wine, and anoints him crosswise on the forehead, nostrils, cheeks, lips, breast and hands, uttering the while the sacramental words, "Holy Father, physician of souls and bodies, do Thou heal thy servant *N.* of the spiritual and bodily infirmities which possess him and quicken him with the grace of Thy Christ." After the seventh anointment, the patient rises up and stands in the midst of the priests, or, if he is unable to rise, the priests come and stand around his bed. Then the senior priest takes the Gospel, opens and holds it, text downward, as it were Christ's own hand, upon the patient's head and recites a prayer for the remission of his sins. The patient kisses the Gospel, and, after hearing the dismissal, asks a blessing of the priests, "Bless, holy fathers, me, a sinner."

The Sacrament of Holy Unction is administered to persons suffering from severe illness; but it is not necessary that the patient should have reached utter exhaustion or unconsciousness. This sacrament may be administered more than once. One to whom health has been restored after receiving Holy Unction is not pledged thereby (as some have mistakenly averred) to renounce the world, to take monastic vows, and to devote the rest of his days to perpetual penance and fasting.

HOLY UNCTION PUBLICLY ADMINISTERED
In the Church of the Dormition at Moscow, on Holy Thursday before the Liturgy, the bishop administers Holy Unction to persons perhaps

healthy in body, but morally suffering from spleen, despondency, and desirous of receiving it in view of the uncertainty of the hour of death. The bishop consecrates the oil and pours some red wine into it. Then follows the readings from the Epistles and the Gospels. Of the prayers only the seventh is recited. After that the bishop stirs the oil and wine with the sacramental spoon, pours out the mixture into small vessels, then anoints on the forehead first himself, then the priests and deacons, then distributes the vessels among the priests, who anoint the people. When this is done, the bishop recites the prayer for the remission of sins while the priests hold over his head the open Gospel text downward.

In the present time, the practice of the public administration of Holy Unction at some time during Great Lent, according, more or less, to the full rite of the sacrament, is also followed in many places.

Molebens

A *moleben* is a special service, in which prayers of thanksgiving and petition are offered to the Lord, to the Mother of God and to the Saints, on occasion of some special occurrence in the life of the nation or of individuals. *Moleben* is a Slavonic word signifying "a service of petition."

Molebens belong either to public or to private worship. Under the head of "public worship" come molebens performed: (1) on "imperial anniversaries," i.e., on the birthdays and names' days of members of the Imperial House, on the day of the accession to the throne of the reigning Emperor, the day of the coronation of their Imperial Majesties; (2) on the day of a temple-feast, i.e., the day sacred to the commemoration of the person or event in whose name and honor a given parish church has been named and dedicated; (3) on days commemorating victories over enemies; (4) on occasions of public calamities, such as foreign invasion, epidemics, pestilence, drought or excessive rains, and the like. To "private worship" belong molebens performed at the desire of private persons on their birthdays and name's days, before children begin lessons, when any one starts on a journey, when a new dwelling is entered, when thanks are given for some mercy which had been prayed for, for the recovery of a sick person, etc.

Molebens are of three kinds: one includes the singing of a canon, another omits the canon, and the third omits the Gospel lesson.

THE ORDER OF THE MOLEBEN WITH A CANON
The order of the moleben with a canon is as follows: after the preliminary exclamation by the priest, "O Heavenly King..." is sung, then the Trisagion and the Lord's Prayer; after that a psalm is read, selected with reference to the object prayed for. After the psalm the Great Ectenia is

recited, with the addition of petitions bearing on the occasion of the moleben. Then are sung: "God is the Lord...," troparia and the Penitential Psalm "Have mercy on me, O God...," and at last the canon with refrains in the honor of the person invoked. For instance, in a canon to the Holy Trinity, the refrain is, "Most Holy Trinity, our God, glory to Thee"; in a canon to the Virgin, it is, "Most-holy Mother of God, save us"; in a canon to St. Nicholas, it is, "Father and Bishop Nicholas, pray to God for us."

After the third ode of the canon, the Triple Ectenia is recited; after the sixth ode, the Small Ectenia, which is followed by the reading from the Gospel (if the moleben is in honor of two or more Saints, two or more Gospels are read); after the ninth ode the hymn "It is truly meet..." is sung. This is followed by the Trisagion, the Lord's Prayer, and the Triple Ectenia, after which a special prayer is read, appropriate to the object of petition or thanksgiving. Thus, a moleben with canon is—in its order—an abbreviation of Matins. An akathist is sometimes joined with the canon, when it is recited after the sixth ode, before the Gospel lesson. Molebens with canons are sung on temple-feasts in honor of the Lord and His Saints, for deliverance from foes, in times of excessive rain, drought, or epidemic.

The Order of the Moleben without a Canon
The moleben without a canon proceeds in the same manner until the hymn "God is the Lord." After that and the troparia, readings from the Epistles and Gospel are read (sometimes a paremia is read before the Epistle); the Gospel lesson is followed by the Triple Ectenia, after which the priest recites the special prayer for the occasion, which is listened to kneeling, and the Great Doxology is sung. Sometimes a prayer for the granting of length of days to the Emperor and his House is said after the Doxology. Molebens of this kind are sung on New Year's Day, on the anniversary of the reigning Emperor's accession to the throne and of the Coronation, to give thanks for some great mercy, for the safety of the Emperor and the soldiers in battle, on occasion of a child's first lesson, for

recovery from sickness, to ask a blessing on those that depart on journeys or to navigate the waters, and on bee-hives, and other sundry objects.

THE GOSPEL READING

There is no Gospel reading when the object of the moleben is to ask a blessing on various inanimate objects, such as a war vessel, an army flag, arms or ordnance, a new ship or boat, or on the digging of a well, or finding of water, or a newly completed well. All such articles are sprinkled with holy water, hence to the moleben is joined the rite of the Lesser Consecration of Water, which is performed after the model of the consecration prescribed for the 1st of August.

The Order of the Consecration (Tonsure) of a Monk

The name of *Monk* (or *Nun*) is given to persons who have taken the vows of chastity, poverty, and absolute obedience to the will of their spiritual guides, with complete surrender of their own will. Monks live together in separate buildings, called Monasteries or *Lavras*.[61] There each monk has a place to himself, which is called a *cell*. They assemble all together only in the church, for services, in the refectory and at their common work. They are called to be in perfect subordination to the will of their chief, the Father Superior of the monastery, who has the title of *Hegúmen* (a Greek word which means "leader," and refers to an abbot) or of Archimandrite (another Greek word which means "chief of a fold"). At the present time ,all abbots and archimandrites have the dignity of priesthood but this was not always the case in ancient times. A monastery may also be headed by a bishop. Monks are divided into three grades: that of *novices, monks of the lesser vows*, and *of the highest vows*. Persons who desire to take on themselves monastic vows do not at once enter the ranks of monks; they are first subjected to tests to prove the firmness of their intent. In other words, they pass through the "ordeal of obedience," sometimes lasting several years, during which they are on probation, and therefore are called probationers or lay brethren. Both these and the novices are under the special guidance of an older monk, of their own choice, who is called a *stárets* (a Russian word, meaning "elder"). As one of the acts of a monk's consecration consists in cutting or tonsuring his hair, the ceremony is also called *tonsure*. There is a special order of consecration for every grade of monastic life.

MONASTIC GARMENTS

1. The Robe (*Riássa*).
2. The Prayer Rope.
3. The *Klóbuk*.
4. The Mantle, or *Pallium*.
5. The Cowl (*Cucullus*) of the Great Schema.
6. A Bishop's Mantle.
7. The Belt.
8. The *Analavon* of the Great Schema.
9. The *Paramand*.

According to the ancient canons, a monk may also live as a *hermit*, or with one or two others separate from a monastery, but only after he has completed many years of life in a monastery, and has demonstrated perfect obedience, and received a blessing from the Superior to live apart.

The Order of Investing With the Robe

After the prefatory prayers and penitential troparia, the abbot recites a prayer wherein he asks the Lord to vouchsafe that the probationer who desires to enter monastic life may acquit himself worthily in the angelic state[62] and to admit him into the flock of His elect; then he tonsures the hair on the novice's head in the form of a Cross,[63] "in the name of the Father, and the Son, and the Holy Spirit," in token that he, the novice, "casts from him all idle thoughts and acts and takes upon himself the yoke of the Lord." After the tonsuring, the abbot invests him with the garb of his order, the robe (*riássa*) and the *kamilavka* or skull-cap, both black and of inexpensive material. The robe is a wide garment, unbelted, such as was worn in ancient times on days of sorrowing; the monk dons "cap protecting from the heat," or "allaying heat") betokens the taming of the passions. By assuming the robe, the probationer enters the ranks of the "newly-consecrated" or novices, and receives the title of *riássophor,* i.e., "wearer of the robe," but takes no vows.

The Order of the Lesser Schema

The word *Schema* means "dignity, aspect"; the "Order of the Lesser Schema" is the name given to the consecration of a novice into the second grade of monastic life, that of monk proper. This rite generally takes place in church, before the Liturgy or after Matins. The novice who wishes to take the vows removes his garments on the porch, in token that he renounces all wrongdoing, and stands unbelted, unshod, and bareheaded. Then the brethren (i.e., the community of the monastery) come forth from the church to fetch him, with lighted candles, chanting a troparion which celebrates the return of the prodigal son to his father's house, and conduct him into the church. The novice performs three prostrations on the way, stops opposite the royal gates, before a lectern on which are laid a Cross and Gospel, and here, to the question of the abbot, who asks him, "Why hast thou come hither, Brother, falling down before the holy altar, and before this holy assembly?" he replies, "I am desirous of the life of asceticism, Reverend Father (or holy Master)." Then the abbot questions him further: whether he aspires to the angelic state, whether he gives himself to God of his own free will, whether he intends to abide in the monastery and lead a life of mortification unto his last breath, whether he intends to keep himself in the observance of virginity, chastity and piety, whether he will remain obedient to the superior and to the brethren unto death? Whether he will endure willingly the restraint and hardships of monastic life. When he has answered to all these questions, "Yea, reverend Father, with the help of God," the abbot explains to him wherein monastic life consists. He pledges himself to keep his vows. Then the abbot prays that "the Lord may receive him, shield him by the operation of the Holy Spirit and deliver him from all carnal lusts," and, laying his hand on the Gospel adds, "Here Christ is present invisibly. Behold! No one compels thee to come to Him." Then, the better to test his willingness to take the vows, he hands him the shears thrice, with the words, "Take these shears and give them to me." The novice every time receives the shears and returns them to the abbot, kissing his hand. After the third time, the abbot says to him, "From the hand of Christ thou didst receive them. Behold to Whom thou joinest thyself, Whom thou embracest, and whom thou renouncest." Then the abbot tonsures the novice's head in the form of a Cross, saying, "Our brother (or our sister) cuts the hair of his (or her) head in the name of the Father, and the Son, and the Holy Spirit," and in doing so, changes his (or her) name for another, in token of complete renunciation of the world[64] and perfect self-consecration to God.

The recipient of the Schema is now invested with the garb of his order. He dons a *chiton*, usually called runic or cassock, as an emblem of poverty (in ancient times this tunic was made of horsehair), then he puts on an article called *paramand*, which means "something besides, or added to the mantle." This name is given to a square of cloth, on which is represented the Cross of Christ with the spear, the reed, and the inscription, "I wear upon my body the wounds of my Lord." By means of strings sewed to the corners, this square is fastened around the shoulders and waist of the monk. It is intended to remind him that he has taken on himself the yoke of Christ and must control his passions and desires. At the same time, a Cross is hung on his neck, in token that he is to follow Christ. Over these the monk puts on the robe, which is now called "the robe of rejoicing," and girds himself with the belt, in token of spiritual regeneration and mortification of the body. Over the robe, the monk is invested with the *pallium* or mantle, a wide garment, very long and without sleeves. It is called "the garment of incorruption and purity," and the absence of sleeves is to remind the monk that he is debarred from worldly pursuits. The mantle is given him in token of the "exalted angelic state" which he assumes, i.e., as a pledge that he will not stop on this second grade, but will seek the third, highest. The head-gear given to him is the kamilávka with the *klóbuk* or veil, which is to remind him that he must veil his face from temptation, and guard his eyes and ears against all vanity. Therefore, the klóbuk is called the "helmet of salvation." The feet of the monk are shod with sandals (shoes), in token that he should abide in peace and calm, and be slow in pursuing his own wishes or doing his own will. Lastly, he is given a prayer rope or *"chôtki"* ("counter"), i.e., a cord with many knots, to count prayers and prostrations by. This counter is the monk's spiritual sword which helps him to conquer absentmindedness while at prayers, by which he drives evil counsel from his soul. Sometimes the prayer rope consists of small metallic plates strung on a string or rope, at equal intervals; it is then called by a name which means "small ladder" *(lyestófka)* because it looks like one.

After the vesting, the Great Ectenia is recited, with the addition of special petitions on behalf of the new brother, and the prokimenon is sung, "As many as have been baptized into Christ, have put on Christ;" then readings: from the Epistles how that every man must wage war against the foes of salvation, and invest himself to that end with the full panoply of God; and from the Gospel, how that the love of God must be greater than the love of parents, and how he that does not follow in the footsteps of the Lord is unworthy of Him. Then the new brother is presented with a candle and a Cross, and reminded of the words of Christ, that whoever would follow Him must take up his Cross, and glorify his Heavenly Father by his good deeds. Lastly, the abbot and all the brethren give him the kiss of welcome.

THE ORDER OF THE GREAT SCHEMA, OR HIGHEST ANGELIC STATE

Those monks who take upon themselves the Great Schema are called in Russian, *Schémniks*. They take severer vows of complete renunciation of the world. The consecration for this highest grade differs from that of the lesser grade in the following points: (1) the vestments prepared for the candidate are taken into the Sanctuary the evening before and laid upon the altar, to signify that he receives them from the Lord Himself; (2) his name is again changed at his consecration; (3) in the place of the paramand, he puts on the *analavon*, which answers to the paramand, but is ornamented with many Crosses and worn on the shoulders, to signify the bearing of his Cross in following Christ; (4) instead of the flat-topped klóbuk, he puts on a pointed cap called a cowl (*cucullus*), with veil covering the head and shoulders and decorated with five Crosses: on the brow, the breast, the shoulders and the back. It is called "the cowl of guilelessness" and "the helmet of hope in salvation."

CONSECRATION OF AN ABBOT OR ARCHIMANDRITE

When a monk is consecrated for abbot (Father Superior), he is given a pastoral staff emblematic of his duty as ruler of the community. If he is consecrated for the dignity of an archimandrite, he is invested with a mantle which has four squares of red or green cloth called tables of the law sewed on in front, at the neck and at the bottom. They signify that the archimandrite is the monk's instructor and guide in living in accordance with the commandments of God. Bishops, who at the present time are taken from among the archimandrites, wear mantles, not black, but of some light color with stripes of another color which begin at the neck and run all around the mantle down to the skirt. These stripes are called "rivers" and signify that from the bishop's lips flow rivers of instruction in the Word of God.

The Burial
and Commemoration
of the Dead

THE PRAYERS FOR A DEPARTING SOUL

The Orthodox Church bestows on the dying a blessing and a parting word to ease their passage into life eternal at the moment of the separation of the soul from the body. This parting word consists of a prayerful canon to our Lord Jesus Christ and to His Immaculate Mother. The troparia of this canon express, on behalf of the dying person, the consciousness of sin, the fear of punishment, and the hope in the intercession of the Mother of God and in the mercy of Christ. The canon ends with a prayer that the Lord may remit the dying person's sins and grant his soul rest with the saints in the eternal abodes.

THE PREPARATION OF A DECEASED CHRISTIAN'S BODY
FOR BURIAL

After death, a Christian's body is washed and clothed in new garments. The latter either are all white, when they are called a shroud or winding-sheet, and refer to the promise which the deceased gave at baptism to lead a life of purity and holiness; or else they are the garments of his rank and dignity in life, in token that he must render an account to God of the manner in which he acquitted himself of the duties of the position to which he was called. On his brow is placed a band on which are represented Christ, His Mother and John the Baptist, with the words of the Trisagion, in token that the deceased, as a warrior of Christ, contended on earth for the truth and died with the hope of receiving a crown in Heaven. In the hands is placed an icon of the Saviour or of some Saint, symbolizing the deceased's faith in Christ and his wish to be admitted into the community of holy disciples. Then the body is laid in a coffin and covered with a pall to signify that the deceased is under the shelter of the Church of Christ.

THE READING OF THE PSALTER BY THE COFFIN
AND THE REQUIEM SERVICES

Immediately after a Christian's death, the reading of the Psalter begins by his coffin, with the addition, after each "Glory" (stasis or antiphon), of prayers for the rest of his soul, and Requiem services are celebrated, called *pannychída*, which means, "an all-night service." But they are in reality only short services, consisting of petitions for the forgiveness of the deceased's sins, and for rest for his soul in the Kingdom of Heaven. This service is an abbreviation of Matins. It begins with the reading or chanting of Psalm 90: "He that dwelleth in the help of the Most High, shall abide under the shelter of the God of Heaven."

Then follows the Great Ectenia, with an added petition for the departed; after which are sung: "Alleluia," troparia with the refrain, "Blessed Art Thou, O Lord," the Penitential Psalm, the canon with three Small Ecteniæ after the third, sixth and ninth odes, the Trisagion, the Lord's Prayer, funeral troparia, the Triple Ectenia, and Dismissal, proclaiming "Memory Eternal" of the departed. During the Requiem, the coffin is censed all around, to signify that the soul of the departed, like unto the fumes from the censer, ascendeth to heaven and that our prayers for him are pleasing to God. This service bears the name of an "all-night service," because, in ancient times, at the funeral of martyrs, the Christians used to spend the entire night, chanting and praying.

THE BEARING FORTH OF THE BODY TO THE CHURCH

The body is taken to a church before burial. Just before it is borne forth from the house, a short service, called *Litý* is held—an abbreviated Requiem—consisting of troparia, the Triple Ectenia and Dismissal.

The coffin is again censed all around during this service. The body of the departed brother is carried to the church to the chanting of the Trisagion, in token that the departed now passeth into the abode of the celestial hosts, there to sing with them the hymn to the Holy Trinity. The Christians who surround the coffin hold lighted candles in their hands, thereby expressing the certainty that their departed brother ascendeth into eternal light, which is God. The coffin is placed in the middle of the church, facing the Sanctuary, and lights are lit all around it.

THE FUNERAL SERVICE

The entire funeral rite is inspired by prayer for the departed and the desire to console the survivors. It begins with the chanting of Psalms 90 and 118, which set forth the blessedness of them that have lived trusting in the help of the Most High and in the observance of His law. Then, after "Alleluia" has been sung thrice, follow troparia with the refrain, "Blessed art Thou, O Lord; teach me Thy statutes." In these troparia man's entire lot is pictured. Created from nothing, but endowed with the likeness of God, he returns to earth for having transgressed the divine commandment; yet, notwithstanding that he bears upon himself the wounds of sin, he still retains the image of the ineffable glory of God, and dares to beseech the merciful Lord for restoration to his glorious home. The troparia are followed by the singing of the funeral canon, containing prayers for the departed; after the third, sixth and ninth odes, the Small Ectenia is recited. Then are sung the *Idoméla*: these are eight stichera, which contain the lamentations of man, who realizes how fleeting and perishable are earthly things. Each stichera is sung to a tone or melody of its own (as indicated by the name, *idoméla*: "their own melodies").

> What earthly sweetness remaineth unmixed with sorrow? What glory on earth continueth unchanged? All things are more feeble than shadows, all things are more deceptive than dreams ... Where is worldly inclination? Where the imaginings of the ephemeral creatures of a day? Where are the gold and the silver? Where is the multitude of servants and noise? All is dust, all ashes, all a shadow. . . . I weep and lament, when I think about death, and see our beauty, fashioned according to God's

image, lying in the grave, disfigured, without glory, bereft of form. O marvel! What is this mystery concerning us? How have we been given up to corruption? How have we been linked with death? Truly, as it is written, by the command of God, Who giveth repose unto the departed.[65]

After the stichera, the Beatitudes are chanted; then there are readings from the Epistles and Gospel, which speak of the resurrection of the dead, and give comfort to them that mourn over the vanity of all earthly things.

The readings from Scripture are followed by the Ectenia of Supplication, which concludes with the "prayer of absolution," in which the Church remits all the departed's transgressions, absolves him from all obligations, all pledges or oaths, and sends him off in peace into life everlasting. In token that the prayers of the Church have weight with God and that what is remitted to the penitent on earth is remitted to them in heaven also, it is customary in our country to place in the departed's hands a paper with this prayer written upon it.

The funeral service ends with the singing of sticheræ, which speak of the separation of our departed brother from us and express his request that we should pray for him. This is the moment when the last kiss is given and the coffin is closed; then "memory eternal" of the departed is proclaimed.

Burial, or Laying the Body in the Grave
When the funeral service is concluded, the coffin is lowered into the grave, facing the East, to signify that the deceased is going towards the Orient of life everlasting, to await the second coming of Christ, the Sun of Truth. While the coffin is being lowered, the prayers of the Litia are chanted; then the priest casts earth crosswise upon the coffin, saying, "The earth is the Lord's and the fullness thereof, the world and all that dwell therein," and pours oil upon it, if the departed received holy unction in life, and also scatters on it ashes from the censer. This oil,

unused for the lamp, and these extinct ashes symbolize the life which has been extinguished on earth, but is—by God's mercy—to be resurrected for everlasting bliss.

Christian graves are dug either in a cemetery by a church, or within the church building, to signify that they who have been true to the Church in life, are sheltered by her in death.

PRAYERS AND RITES AFTER THE BURIAL

The Church cares for Christians in death. She prays for them and offers the Bloodless Sacrifice of the Liturgy in their behalf on the third, ninth and fortieth day after their decease, then every year on the anniversary of death, which is called the "day of remembrance" or "commemoration." On the third day, we pray that Christ, Who rose from the dead on the third day after His death, may resurrect our departed brother into a life of blessedness; on the ninth day, we pray the Lord that He may number the departed among the nine orders of Angels and Saints; on the fortieth day, we beseech Christ that He Who endured temptation from the devil on the fortieth day of His fast may help the departed to stand the ordeal of God's judgment without being shamed, and that He Who ascended to Heaven on the fortieth day, may receive the departed into the heavenly abode. Sometimes he is commemorated daily through all the forty days, by the celebration of the Liturgy in memory of him. By devoting to prayer the anniversary day of our brother's demise, we express the belief that the day of a man's death is not the day of his annihilation, but of his birth into life everlasting.

At all commemorative services is set forth a dish of boiled wheat or rice with honey *(Kólivo* or *Kutyá)*. The grain symbolizes resurrection, while the honey (or sugar) indicates the sweet, blissful life in the Kingdom of Heaven.

Apart from private commemorations of every deceased Christian, at the wish of his friends and relatives, there are certain days set apart by the Church for the commemoration of all deceased Christians generally. The church services for these days are called "Universal Requiems," and the days themselves are called "ancestral days" (All-Souls'). Such days are: the Saturday before Cheese-Fare week; the Saturdays of the second, third and fourth weeks in Lent; the Saturdays before Trinity (Pentecost) and before the feast of St. Dimitri of Thessalonica (26th of October); the Tuesday—in some localities the Monday—of St. Thomas' week (the week after Pascha); and the day of the Beheading of John the Baptist. The Saturday before St. Dimitri's feast was instituted in memory of the Great-Prince Dimitri Donskoy and of the warriors killed on the Field of Kulikof in the great battle against the Tatars.

Special Features of the Burial of Priests and Babes

The body of a priest is not washed, but sponged with pure oil and clothed in the sacred vestments. The face is covered with an aër, and in the hands are placed a Cross and Gospel. The body is borne to the church in procession, the church bells ringing a carillon. Before every church which the procession passes, the Litý service is performed. During the funeral service, five readings from the Epistles and five from the Gospels are read; after the funeral canon, the sticheræ on "Praise the Lord" are sung, then the Great Doxology. More idiomela are sung than at the funerals of laymen.

For babes who have died after receiving baptism,[66] the funeral service is performed after a special rite, the Church praying not that the departed's sins be forgiven him, but that the Lord, according to His unfailing promise, may vouchsafe to receive him, as being blessed and undefiled, into the Kingdom of Heaven.

Books Containing the Divine Service

The Order of divine service, both public and private, is contained in special books, some of which give the daily service, and others the order of the various ministrations.

Under the former heading come: the *Clergy Service Book*, the *Bishop's Service Book*, the *Horologion*, the *Oktoëchos*, the *Monthly Menaion*, the *Feast-day Menaion*, the *Common Menaion*, the *Lenten Triodion*, the *Pentecostarion*, the *Eirmologion*, and the *Typicon*.

The Clergy Service Book *(Sluzhébnik)* contains the unalterable prayers and ceremonies of Matins, Vespers and the Liturgy, performed by the priest and the deacon. The Bishop's Service Book *(Chinóvnik)* is the Pontifical Book of Offices, differing from the other in that it contains all the prayers and ceremonies in use at pontifical services; also the Order of Ordination and Consecration for all grades and dignities of the church. The *Horológion (Chasoslóv)* contains the unalterable prayers of the daily services recited and chanted by the readers and choristers. The *Oktoëchos*, the *Menéœ* ,the *Triódia* and the *Eirmológion* contain the changeable prayers and compositions in use in the daily services. The *Oktoëchos* (which means the "Book of Eight Tones") contains the changeable songs of praise of the weekly cycle of services. The name of the book comes from this— hat the services of the entire week are sung in one "tone," and the "tones" are eight in number. In the monthly *Menéœ*, we find the changeable prayers appointed for each day of the 12 months; it is therefore divided into 12 parts. The Feast-day *Menaion* contains the prayers for the feasts of the Lord, of the Mother of God and of the more honored Saints, selected from the Monthly *Meneœ*. In the Common *Menaion* we find the prayers prescribed in the services in honor of all the Saints of the different orders—apostles, martyrs, hierarchs. The *Triodion* (which means the "book of three songs") contains the changeable prayers for the moveable days of the yearly cycle of services, and in the *Triodes* (the numbers), i.e., incomplete canons, consisting of two, three, or four odes. There are two *Triodiœ*: the Lenten (*Triodion*), giving the services for Lent and the preparatory weeks thereto, and the *Festal (Menaion)* for the feast days of the liturgical year, and the *Pentecostarion* gives the services from Easter Sunday to the All-Saints' Week. In the *Eirmologion* we find the prayers which are sung—not read or recited—at the various services. This book has its name from the fact that it contains, among others, the *eirmoi* of the canons. The Order of the service for each day of the year is given in the book called *Typicon* (which means "statute").

The services performed by private desire are described in the *Book of Needs* (or "of Ministrations"), in the *Order for the Reception into the Church of Members of Alien Creeds,* and in the *Book of Chants.*

Some books belong to both private and public worship. Such are the Gospels, the Epistles, and the Psalter. The former two are divided into readings, with the indication of the lesson for each day. The Psalter is divided into twenty kathismata, with each, in turn, divided into three "Glories." The Psalter is sometimes printed in one volume with the Horologion. It is then called "A Psalter with Sequence."

There is still another class of books, which contain extracts from other books, and are meant for private home use, such as: the *Book of Rules,* which tells how to prepare for Communion, and gives the services and prayers required by these rules; the books "of collected Akathists," and "of collected canons"; the "Book of Saints," giving the troparia and kontakia for each day; and the "Euchologion" (Prayer Book), complete or abridged.

The end, and glory be to God.

Notes

1 Thus for instance, on the spot where Christ rose from the dead was built the church of the Resurrection; in St. Petersburg we have the church named for the Venerable Isaac of Dalmatia, because Peter the Great, the founder of the city, was born on that Saint's day.

2 We call "Gospel," the book which contains the narrative of the earthly life of Christ our Saviour, and His teachings. It consists of four books written by the Apostles Matthew, Mark, Luke and John. The Greek word *Evangélion* means "Good News." The description of Christ's earthly life is thus named, because it brings us the good news of our salvation. Hence, the Apostles, who have written the Saviour's Life, are named "Evangelists," which means "bringers of good news."

3 Jerusalem was the ancient capital of the Hebrews; Sion was a mountain near Jerusalem on which were built the palaces of David and Solomon. Christians began to give these names to the kingdom of Heaven, which they hoped to reach through Christ, Who suffered for the sins of men near the earthly Jerusalem, and, later on, to the tabernacles in which the Holy Gifts are kept, through partaking of which in communion they hoped to receive salvation.

4 Christ is represented in royal garments, because He is the King Who founded the Kingdom of God on earth, and in episcopal vestments because He is the High-Priest Who offered Himself in sacrifice for the sins of man. The name of *Deisis* given to such an icon is derived from the Greek word Deisis, which means "prayer." It is probable that in ancient times a prayer was written below the icon, probably with the heading: "Deisis" and men, ignorant of the Greek tongue, took the word for the name of the icon.

5 The events in commemoration of which these feasts were established are known from Sacred History; therefore, they are not related here. The entire narrative of the finding of the Holy Cross belongs to the history of the Church.

6 *Prayer Book,* Fourth Edition—Revised (Jordanville, New York: Holy Trinity Publications, 2005) pp. 157, 159, 162.

7 A *troparion* is a brief hymn on the nature of the event commemorated or on the labors of the person in whose honor the service is performed, also on the meaning of the service. Every service and every day has its own troparion.

8 The *kontakion* is a short hymn, similar in substance to the troparion, but differing from it in that it develops more amply some one part of the troparion, as for instance this or that particular deed of the Saint of the day, or some one feature of the day's feast.

9 If the service is done without the assistance of a deacon, all that a deacon should do (except asking the blessing of the priest to perform his deacon's duties) is done by the priest.

10 The present formulation reflects the usage of the Russian Orthodox Church Outside Russia in 2001. In Imperial Russia, the petitions were as follows:

"For the Most Holy Governing Synod" (*i.e., the body of bishops and presbyters or priests who govern the Church*), "for our Bishop N., . . . and for all the Clergy and people"; "for our most pious sovereign, the Emperor, and the entire reigning House" (*the Imperial family*), "all the Palace" (*the functionaries appointed by the Tsar*), "and the Army"; "that He may aid them and put down beneath their feet every enemy and adversary," (*i.e., that the Lord may aid them in all things, and subdue their enemies, open or secret, and their adversaries*); etc.

11 At present, the evening kathisma is sung only at Sunday and feast-day Great Vespers. On all other days and almost always at Matins, the kathismata are read, and only the "Glories" are sung.

12 The Unabbreviated Horologion or Book of the Hours (Jordanville, New York: Holy Trinity Monastery, 1997) pp.190–192.

13 *Prayer Book*, Fourth Edition—Revised (Jordanville, New York: Holy Trinity Publications, 2005) p. 68.

14 Thus, the Prokimenon for Sunday Vespers is: "The Lord is King; He is clothed with majesty."

15 More paremia are prescribed for some days than for others. Thus *five* are read at Vespers before the Annunciation, *eight* on the vigil of Christmas day, *twelve* on the vigil of the Epiphany, and *fifteen* on the Saturday before Pascha Sunday.

16 Today, countires that do not have a Christian Emperor have petititons such as this one: "…for this land, its authorities and armed forces. Grant them, O Lord, peaceful governance, that in their calm we also may lead a quiet and

peaceful life in all piety and purity." *The Divine Liturgy of Our Father Among the Saints John Chrysostom* (Jordanville, New York: Holy Trinity Monastery, 2022) p. 187.

17 *Prayer Book*, Fourth Edition—Revised (Jordanville, New York: Holy Trinity Publications, 2005) p.69.

18 *The Unabbreviated Horologion or Book of the Hours* (Jordanville, New York: Holy Trinity Monastery, 1997) pp. 61–62

19 Sion: the mountain on which stood the palace of David and the Tabernacle containing the Ark of the Covenant. "Haters of Sion" are the foes of the people of Israel, or, in Christian speech — of Christianity.

20 *The Unabbreviated Horologion or Book of the Hours* (Jordanville, New York: Holy Trinity Monastery, 1997) p. 62

21 *Prayer Book and Psalms,* Pocket Edition (Jordanville, New York: Holy Trinity Publications, 2019) p. 75.

22 These ecteniæ are distinguished by differences in the Exclamations uttered by the priest. The first celebrates God as the Creator and Divine Providence: "For Thou art our God"; the second—as the Saviour: "For Thou art the King of peace and the Saviour of our souls"; the third—as King of the whole world, visible and invisible: "For all the hosts of Heaven praise Thee."

23 At Sunday Matins the following Theotokion is sung: "Most blessed art thou, O Virgin Theotokos, for through Him Who became incarnate of thee is Hades led captive, Adam recalled, the curse annulled, Eve set free, death slain, and we are given life. Wherefore, we cry aloud in praise: Blessed art Thou, O Christ God, Who hast been thus well-pleased, glory to Thee."

24 *The Unabbreviated Horologion or Book of the Hours* (Jordanville, New York: Holy Trinity Monastery, 1997) pp. 77–78

25 Ibid. p. 92.

26 Ibid. pp. 146–147, 149.

27 On weekdays, we sing "O Son of God, Who art wondrous in the saints..."; on feasts of the Theotokos, "O Son of God, through the prayers of the Theotokos...."

28 *The Divine Liturgy of Our Father Among the Saints John Chrysostom*: Slavonic-English Parallel Text, 5th Edition (Jordanville, New York: Holy Trinity Publications, 2022) p. 141.

29 Formerly, the first petitions were for the reigning Tsar and his House, followed by petitions for the Church authorities, etc.

30 Notwithstanding the reverence with which Christians should receive the Elements at the Great Entry, the Church regulations forbid prostrations at this moment, that infidels may have no occasion to say that Christians adore bread and wine as they do God.

31 In ancient times, the faithful, at these words, embraced and kissed, with the mutual greeting, "Christ is in the midst of us" — "He is and will be," but in the course of time not all preserved the Christian brotherly love; besides, many forgot that Christ is in their midst at this moment; so the ancient custom is now dispensed with, and is observed only by the celebrants at the altar.

32 The words, "singing, shouting, crying aloud, and saying," mean that we should sing the glory of God jointly with those higher angels, who surround the throne of God—those angels whom the Prophet Ezekiel saw in his vision, in the shape of four animals having four faces: an eagle's, a bull's, a lion's, and a man's. As these faces are merely symbols of the spiritual qualities or forces of the angels, the praise uttered in the voices of the four angelic faces is uttered with all the forces of the soul.

33 *Hosanna* is a Hebrew word which means "God save" or "help." "Hosanna in the highest" means either "Hosanna to the Most High" or "May our good wishes be heard in the highest abodes (in Heaven)."

34 The blood of the Old testament is the blood of animals, which were offered in sacrifice and were the prototype of Christ. But the blood of the New Testament is the Blood of Christ, shed for our salvation. Because the wine offered at the Liturgy is mystically transmuted into the Blood of Christ, therefore the New testament sacrifice is called "the Bloodless Sacrifice."

35 Formerly, the Tsar and his house were commemorated first.

36 Ibid. pp. 213–215.

37 *Prayer Book,* Fourth Edition—Revised (Jordanville, New York: Holy Trinity Publications, 2005) p. 157.

38 Ibid. p. 159.

39 Vespers and Liturgy are combined in the following manner: after the Hours, Vespers begins with a blessing on the Reign of the Holy Trinity, then follows the Vespers Entry with the Gospel, after which the prokimenon is sung and paremia recited; these are followed by the Small Ectenia which concludes with the exclamation, "For holy art Thou, O our God"; then the Choir sings the Trisagion, the Epistle is read, and the Gospel; thereafter the Liturgy proceeds as usual.

40 Ibid. p. 160.

41 *Prayer Book and Psalms,* Pocket Edition (Jordanville, New York: Holy Trinity Publications, 2019) p. 55.

42 If the vigil for the Prophet and Forerunner, John the Baptist, happens on any day from Monday to Friday inclusive, the service on the eve of the feast consists of the Royal Hours and the Liturgy of Basil the Great combined with Vespers. On the day of the feast, the Liturgy of Chrysostom is celebrated. If the vigil happens on a Saturday or Sunday, the Liturgy of Chrysostom is celebrated at the proper time, then Vespers, and, on the day of the feast, the Liturgy of Basil the Great; and the Royal Hours are put back to Friday. The All-night Vigil on the eve of the feast begins with Great Compline.

43 In prayer for the sanctification of the waters, the priest asks the Lord that He may impart unto these waters the blessing of Jordan, so that all who take from it and partake of it may do so unto the cleansing of body and soul, unto healing from passions, unto the sanctification of their homes, and unto every kind of benefit; and that He may sanctify the water and grant unto all who touch it or anoint themselves therewith, sanctification, health, purification, and benediction.

44 *The Unabbreviated Horologion or Book of the Hours* (Jordanville, New York: Holy Trinity Monastery, 1997) p. 264.

45 Ibid.

46 In the prayer for the blessing of the fruit of the vine, the priest asks, "that the Lord may bless them, that they may be to us unto rejoicing, and that He may accept of a gift of these fruits unto the cleansing of our sins." When blessing other first fruit (such as apples), he prays, "that the Lord may receive our gift into His eternal treasury and grant us an abundance of worldly goods."

47 In this prayer of the lesser blessing of the water, the priest asks that, through partaking of this water, and besprinkling therewith, the Lord may send down upon us His benediction, "which washeth away the pollution of the passions."

48 Ibid. p. 66.

49 Ibid. pp. 88, 116–117, 126, 177.

50 Some of the Passion Week hymns of Monday bring before us Joseph, sold by his brothers, as the prototype of Christ; and in the barren fig tree, cursed by the Lord Jesus, we are shown the Jews who betrayed Him and put Him to death. The hymns of Tuesday bid us prepare to meet the Heavenly Bridegroom, who receiveth into His chamber only such as have bridal garments woven of virtues—those who meet Him with the lighted lamp of faith and good deeds, and have not hidden but increased the talents given them by God. The hymns of Wednesday recall the supper at Simon's, at which the sinful woman anointed Christ's feet with myrrh.

51 In some places, in memory of the visible sojourn of Christ upon earth after His resurrection, and of His constant invisible presence among the faithful, the Artos is carried around the church every day during the week of Pascha, prior to being distributed on Saturday, or, as is common nowadays, Sunday.

52 *Prayer Book*, Fourth Edition—Revised (Jordanville, New York: Holy Trinity Publications, 2005) p. 215.

53 Ibid. p.217.

54 The Church rules that a woman shall not partake of Holy Communion until the fortieth day after giving birth to a child, unless she be dangerously sick, even unto death.

55 On a BAPTISM PERFORMED BY A LAYMAN: The right to administer the Sacrament of Baptism belongs to the priests. But in an emergency, when no priest is to be had, and the Candidate for baptism is feeble, and there is danger of his dying before he can be baptized, any layman has the right, and indeed the duty, to perform the rite by thrice repeated immersion, or even by aspersion or by pouring of water on the head, with the words, "the servant (or handmaid) of God N. is baptized in the name of the Father, Amen, and of the Son, Amen, and of the Holy Spirit, Amen." Such a baptism is entirely valid. Later on, the priest does not repeat the rite, but only completes it by saying the omitted prayers and performing the omitted rites, then enters it into the church register.

56 At the consecration of a church, if the holy relics were in the newly built church itself, the bishop takes them on his head, to the singing of troparia in honor of the martyrs, and, having offered the prayer, goes forth and carries them in procession around the church. If this is not possible, the bishop, having taken up the holy relics, places them on a lectern before the western door of the church, or before a curtain hung up temporarily in the place of that door.

57 These hymns at ordination indicate that the person receiving holy orders must, in his life and in the exercise of his functions, follow the example of the martyrs; that his preaching must have for its subject the doctrine of the Holy Trinity and that of the Incarnation of the Son of God from a virgin, which was the foundation of the Church and of the Priesthood.

58 For a picture of an Orlets/Eagle rug, see page 27; for a definition, see page 3.

59 The mutual consent of a man and a woman to enter into matrimony is first made known in the home, to a circle of relatives and acquaintances. On this occasion it is customary to have a moleben sung, for the prosperous completion of the matter undertaken, the betrothal rings are given to the engaged couple, in token of consent to their marriage, and their parents or elders bless them with icons of the Saviour and His Mother. The moleben with the ceremonies of giving the rings and blessing constitute what is usually called "betrothal." But a home betrothal cannot take the place of the betrothal in church, which must all the same be performed immediately before the rite of marriage. The home betrothal is a family matter; the promise is made only before relatives and intimates. In the church betrothal, this promise is affirmed before the entire church.

60 At Holy Unction, the grain, though dry, carries in itself the vital germ of a new plant; thus, a sick man may recover, though dried up by disease, if it

so please God. The grain, when laid in the earth, rots, yet its vital principle revives in a new plant; thus, he who dies of sickness, though given to corruption in the earth, will in due time arise to new life.

61 A *Lavra* is a large monastery, with a great number of inhabitants. A cell is, literally, a cellar, a store-room, or a small chamber.

62 The monastic state is called "angelic" because monks take the vow of renunciation of all things worldly, do not marry, do not acquire or hold property, and live as the angels do in heaven, glorifying God night and day and striving to do His will.

63 At the tonsure of a monk, the abbot cuts a lock of hair from each of the four points of a cross.

64 When changing the name at a tonsure to indicate renuncuation of the world, it is customary to give to monks names which are used seldom or not at all among laymen.

65 *The Funeral Service for The Laity* (Jordanville, New York: Holy Trinity Publications, 2002) p. 68–73.

66 For babes who have died unbaptized, no funeral service is performed, they not having been cleansed of the original sin. Of their future lot, St. Gregory the Theologian says that they will be neither glorified nor punished by the righteous Judge, as such that have not received the seal, yet are not wicked, and have suffered more than done harm, "For not every one who is not deserving of punishment is therefore deserving of honor; nor is every one who is not deserving of honor therefore deserving of punishment."